teach yourself...
CorelDRAW! 5.0

by Dawn Erdos

MIS:
PRESS

A Subsidiary of
Henry Holt and Co., Inc.

First Edition—1994

Erdos, Dawn.

    Teach yourself...CorelDraw! 5.0/Dawn Erdos.
       p.   cm.
    Includes index.
    ISBN 1-55828-375-7 : $21.95
      1. Computer graphics. 2. CorelDraw! I. Title.
  T385.E74   1994   94-34889
  006.6'86—dc20   CIP

Printed in the United States of America.

10 9 8 7 6 5 4 3 2

MIS:Press books are available at special discounts for bulk purchases for sales promotions, premiums, fund-raising, or educational use. Special editions or book excerpts can also be created to specification.

For details contact: Special Sales Director
                        MIS:Press
                        a subsidiary of Henry Holt and Company, Inc.
                        115 West 18th Street
                        New York, New York 10011

Publisher: Brenda McLaughlin   Development Editor: Debra Williams Cauley
Technical Editor: Bud Paulding   Production Editor: Anne Alessi
Copy Editor: Sara Black   Associate Production Editor: Erika Putre

DEDICATION

To Hari Amrit

ACKNOWLEDGMENTS

I would like to extend great appreciation to the following people for their invaluable assistance with this book:

- ❖ Debra Williams Cauley, Development Editor, for keeping this project on track and under control and, as always, for being so flexible.
- ❖ Anne Alessi and Erika Putre for handling the production of this book.
- ❖ Sara Black for a great copy editing job.
- ❖ Rick Wiselus at Computer Wise for providing high-quality equipment and technical support at affordable rates.

Table of Contents

Chapter 1

Introduction:
Entering Your Studio

CorelDRAW is one of the most powerful, versatile, and comprehensive graphics programs on the market today. With it, you can create exciting powerful graphics, incorporate text and graphics from other programs, and provide all types of graphic data to other programs, such as word processors or desktop publishers. This chapter covers:

❖ What Is CorelDRAW

❖ What You Will Learn

❖ Microsoft Windows

❖ Mousing Around

❖ Installing CorelDRAW

❖ Symbols In This Book

❖ Using Help

❖ How To Use This Book

1

What Is CorelDRAW

Actually, the new CorelDRAW, version 5.0, is many different applications and utilities, designed to give you a "studio in a box."

❖ **CorelDRAW**, the heart of the system, is the basic illustration program. With it, you can create graphics and text, manage your files, and import and export files between CorelDRAW and other software. Features in version 5.0 include multiple-page capability, spell checking, other editorial features, style sheets, a graphics database, object linking and embedding, and four-color separations.

❖ **CorelPHOTO-PAINT** is a color image editing and paint program. It gives you a full range of painting and retouching tools and lets you create new bitmapped images and spruce up existing images.

❖ **CorelMOSAIC** helps you find, manage, and manipulate your files, including many different file formats. It gives you thumbnail sketches, or previews, of your data in a visual filing system called a *catalog*. Catalogs allow you to associate files in different locations without moving them around on your drive. CorelMOSAIC performs batch processing for repetitive tasks including printing, importing, exporting, and extract/merge back text operations. Batch operations may be performed from within directories and libraries. CorelMOSAIC also converts files from a photo CD to disk.

❖ **CorelTRACE** traces almost any kind of bitmapped artwork, including scanned data, and turns them into vector-based images. Vector-based images give your artwork smooth lines, not the jagged edges of bitmaps, so you can take advantage of high-quality laser printers and imagesetters. Vector-based images take up less space on your hard disk and print faster than bitmaps. They can also be brought directly into CorelDRAW and manipulated like any other CorelDRAW image.

❖ **CorelSHOW** creates multiple-page presentations, allowing you to import artwork (such as Corel charts) from any Windows application. You can use both animated and still files and add transitional effects between images to create on-screen slideshows. Your presentation can be viewed as an automated screen show, output as a series of slides or overheads, or printed as a publication.

❖ **CorelCHART** develops and displays charts that easily and powerfully express intricate ideas. This powerful data manager lets you enter data and calculate results, and it accepts spreadsheet data from Lotus 1-2-3 and Microsoft Excel. It provides line, bar, and pie charts plus true three-dimensional and other specialized chart types.

❖ **CorelMOVE** is an animation program that simulates the traditional frame-by-frame method. You can create a series of drawings linked together to give an illusion of movement. However, rather than having to draw each cel individually, as in the traditional method, CorelMOVE can create for you intermediary cels in an actors movement. It also allows you to add sound effects and to layer multiple animated images and sounds.

The very features that make CorelDRAW so powerful also make it somewhat difficult to learn without help. The purpose of this book is to help you get started with as little pain and as much fun as possible.

What You Will Learn

You begin learning about CorelDRAW by going over the basics, such as installing CorelDRAW and navigating your way around the screen, via both mouse and keyboard. You'll get a quick overview of the menus and the toolbox options to give you a summary of the functions you can perform. You'll learn about alternate methods and shortcuts, as well as several features designed to make working with CorelDRAW a lot easier.

❖ *Chapter 1* introduces CorelDRAW, describes some of the basic elements of Microsoft Windows, and explains how to install CorelDRAW.

❖ *Chapter 2* describes how to access the CorelDRAW applications and describes the basic elements of the CorelDRAW screen.

❖ *Chapter 3* teaches you how to manage your files on disk, including creating multiple-page documents and importing, exporting, and printing files.

❖ *Chapter 4* covers how to draw lines and curves.

❖ *Chapter 5* helps you manipulate and arrange objects. Topics covered include selecting, moving, copying, deleting, filling, and outlining objects. You also learn how to perform special effects using the Transform menu.

❖ *Chapter 6* describes how to add text to your documents and use CorelDRAW's new editorial features. It also covers special effects as they relate to text, such as wrapping text and placing text on a path.

❖ *Chapter 7* teaches you how to use colors and color palettes in your drawing. You learn how to create custom colors and how to use and customize color palettes.

❖ *Chapter 8* covers special effects including creating perspective and envelopes, blending, extruding, contouring, and drawing power lines.

❖ *Chapter 9* covers the CorelMOSAIC file manager and teaches you how to select, locate, and find files, as well as how to perform batch functions for printing, importing, exporting, and extract/merge back text operations.

❖ *Chapter 10* demonstrates the CorelTRACE utility and shows you how to import, trace, and customize bitmapped images.

❖ *Chapter 11* describes the CorelPHOTO-PAINT program. This chapter teaches you how to use the tools for selecting, displaying, painting, and drawing graphics. It also covers photo retouching techniques, use of filters, and special painting effects.

❖ *Chapter 12* covers the CorelCHART program. You learn how to create a chart, change a chart's appearance, and select various chart types.

❖ *Chapter 13* gives you an overview of CorelSHOW and explains how to create your own presentations for automated screen display, prepare slides or overheads, and print.

❖ *Chapter 14* introduces you to CorelMOVE. You learn basic animation concepts, how to use cel actors and props, and how to combine sound and visual effects to create animation.

❖ *Appendix A* reviews the latest Corel utilities, including CorelKern, CorelQuery, Corel Database Editor, and Template Editor.

❖ *Appendix B* covers all of the keyboard shortcuts for the Corel application modules.

Before we get into CorelDRAW, however, let's discuss some preliminaries— Microsoft Windows (which must be on your computer before you can even install CorelDRAW), the installation process, and how to use CorelDRAW Help.

Microsoft Windows

Microsoft Windows is a graphical user interface (GUI) that allows you to move easily between different applications, and even to pass data between applications. If you haven't yet installed Windows on your system, do so now. You cannot install or use CorelDRAW without it.

Although you can run CorelDRAW with Windows 3.0, you need to install Windows 3.1 to take advantage of all its features. CorelCHART requires Windows 3.1 to run, and certain features of CorelSHOW also require Windows 3.1.

Although you do not need to be a Windows expert to use CorelDRAW, it's a good idea to learn some of the basics first. Try running the *Microsoft Windows Tutorial* or refer to the *Getting Started with Microsoft Windows* manual for an overview.

Windows Basics

To help you out a bit, I'll give you a brief look at the Windows screen to acquaint you with pertinent terminology. Figure 1.1 shows a basic Windows screen.

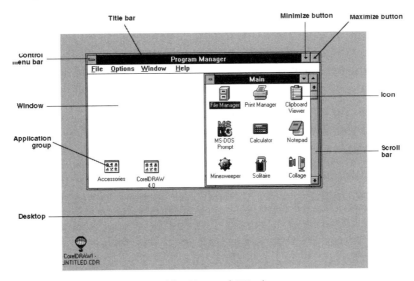

FIGURE 1.1 The Microsoft Windows screen

Let's look at the various elements on the screen.

❖ **Desktop**. The entire screen area.

❖ **Window**. The part of the screen that shows an application or a group of applications.

❖ **Icon**. A pictorial representation or symbol for an application or group.

❖ **Title Bar**. The area containing the name of an application or group.

❖ **Application**. A program that performs a particular function, such as word processing, graphics, or charting—for example, CorelCHART.

❖ **Group**. A collection of applications, such as CorelDRAW or Accessories.

❖ **Minimize Button**. Reduces the application window to an icon.

❖ **Maximize Button**. Enlarges the application window to fill the entire screen.

NOTE

If you maximize a window, the Maximize button is replaced by the Restore button, which is represented by a double-headed arrow. This lets you return the window to its previous size.

❖ **Scroll Bars**. Moves "hidden" parts of a document into view. The screen can have both a horizontal and a vertical scroll bar.

❖ **Control-Menu Box**. Allows you to access the Control menu, which is shown in Figure 1.2. The Control menu contains the following options:

   – **Restore** returns the window to its previous size.

   – **Move** lets you use the arrow keys to move the window.

   – **Size** lets you use the arrow keys to resize the window.

   – **Minimize** reduces the window to an icon.

   – **Maximize** enlarges the window to fill the entire screen.

   – **Close** closes the window or dialog box.

   – **Switch** To allows you to move to another application without closing the current one.

FIGURE 1.2 The Windows Control menu

Mousing Around

Although you can use the keyboard to perform most Windows functions, you'll find that using your mouse is the most efficient way to work in Windows. Let's cover some basic terms.

❖ **Point**. Move the mouse until the screen pointer rests on the item you want.

❖ **Click**. Quickly press and release the mouse button.

❖ **Double-click**. Quickly press and release the mouse button twice.

❖ **Drag** or **click and drag**. Hold down the mouse button while you move the mouse.

Installing CorelDRAW

Installing CorelDRAW 4.0 is a simple but lengthy process. Reserve at least half an hour to install this program. You may want to use your waiting time to thumb through this book and give yourself a quick view of what's in store.

Before you begin, make sure you're prepared. You'll need:

❖ A 386 or 486 computer.

❖ Windows 3.1.

❖ 2M of memory is the minimum, but, as with any graphics application, more is always better. At the beginning of the installation process, CorelDRAW verifies that there is enough memory available before continuing.

❖ A graphic monitor, such as EGA, VGA, or SVGA monitor

❖ A mouse or other pointing device. CorelDRAW also supports pressure-sensitive pen tablets.

To begin the installation, open the Windows Program Manager and select **Run** from the File menu. In the Command Line field of the dialog box, type **A:SETUP** (or **B:SETUP** if you're running the installation from that drive); then click on **OK**.

Simply follow the installation procedure that is displayed on the screen. Setup lets you know when it needs information from you. You can choose to install only portions of the complete package, or you can accept the default installation.

Symbols in This Book

Key combinations are indicated with a hyphen (-) between the keys. For example, **Ctrl-S** (the standard key combination for the Save command) indicates holding down the **Ctrl** key while pressing **S**.

Items of special significance are highlighted throughout the book using the following icons:

Indicates important information, a helpful hint, or special caution.

Indicates a way to save time and effort by following the indicated suggestion.

Indicates a serious warning. Information marked with this icon can prevent loss of data or prevent an action that could result in damage to a disk or to the operation of your system.

Using Help

All of the CorelDRAW 5.0 applications have a Help menu you can access from the menu bar. Click on **Help** or press **F1** to access Help.

The easiest way to use Help is to click on the **Index** option and then browse through the list of topics. To get help for one of the items in the index, double-click on the item, and the information for that topic is displayed on the screen.

If you know exactly what you need help for, select **Search** and type a keyword or phrase. Help displays the available information.

How to Use This Book

To use this book most effectively, follow along on your computer. I've included lots of examples and practice sessions to get you started. Learning computer programs, particularly graphics, is a hands-on task. So, book in hand, mouse poised to run, fingers on the keyboard, teach yourself CorelDRAW.

Chapter 2

The Big Picture: An Overview of CorelDRAW! 5.0

This chapter covers:

- ❖ Starting CorelDRAW
- ❖ The CorelDRAW screen

Starting CorelDRAW

Open CorelDRAW by typing **win** at the DOS prompt and then double-clicking on the Corel Group icon. The CorelDRAW 5.0 window, shown in Figure 2.1, is displayed.

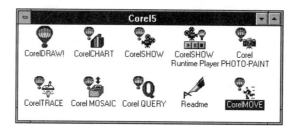

FIGURE 2.1 The CorelDRAW window

Notice that there are many icons in this window, representing different CorelDRAW 5.0 applications. Double-click on the CorelDRAW icon to display its main screen.

The CorelDRAW Screen

The screen, or desktop, contains many elements that allow you to access CorelDRAW's features. Let's cover all the screen elements illustrated in Figure 2.2.

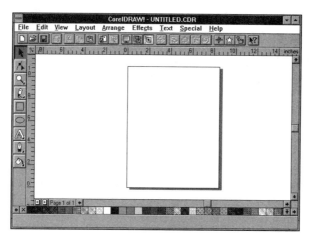

FIGURE 2.2 The CorelDRAW screen

Windows Border and Title Bar

At the very top of the screen is the Windows border and the title bar.

The *Windows border* resizes windows. Place your mouse over the border. When the double arrows are displayed, simply click and drag to reduce or enlarge your window. The Windows border is inactive when a window is maximized.

At the center of the *title bar*, you'll see the title of the program, *CorelDRAW*, and the name of the current file.

Your title bar probably reads *untitled.cdr*. This is because you haven't loaded an existing file or saved the file you are working on. Once you save your drawing as a file and give it a name, the title bar reflects the file name.

The Menu Bar and Ribbon Bar

The next line of Figure 2.2 contains the *menu bar*. You will be using these pull-down menus to manage your files, customize and modify your drawings, and tailor your screen display to your individual preferences. In the following chapters, as we proceed through the Toolbox, we'll take a closer look at some of the options in these menus. Here's a quick overview.

❖ The **File menu** controls the files in and out of CorelDRAW and also manages printing.

❖ The **Edit menu** cuts, copies, pastes, deletes, clones, and links information and reverses your previous action.

❖ The **View menu** controls the way your screen is set up (for example, how your Toolbox is displayed) and your preview modes. It provides on-screen aids such as a ruler, a grid, and preview options. This menu was known as the Display menu in version 4.0.

❖ The **Layout menu** inserts, deletes, goes to, and sets up pages; controls the Layer and Style roll-up menus; and sets grids, guidelines, and snaps.

❖ The **Arrange menu** groups images, breaks apart groups of images, and changes an object's relative position in a drawing.

❖ The **Effects menu** changes the angle, size, rotation, or movement of objects on the screen. It blends, envelopes, adds perspective to, extrudes, and contours objects in your drawing. This menu also controls the power line feature. Many of your roll-up menus are found under the Effects menu.

❖ The **Text menu** edits, aligns, or modifies your text, invokes the spelling checker or thesaurus, finds and replaces text, and fits your text to a path.

❖ The **Special menu** contains miscellaneous options and user preferences, as well as custom features for patterns, arrows, and symbols.

❖ The **Help menu** accesses on-line help for all the CorelDRAW tools and menu options.

Under the menu bar is the *ribbon bar*, a feature new to version 5.0. The ribbon bar allows you to access many menu options without opening a menu; simply click on a button, and you can save, print, cut, paste, preview, and so forth. Figure 2.3 shows what each button does.

FIGURE 2.3 The ribbon bar

The Toolbox

Your *toolbox* contains icons for drawing tools (lines, rectangles, ellipses, and text), editing tools (select, shape, outline, and fill), and viewing tools magnification. The toolbox is illustrated in Figure 2.4.

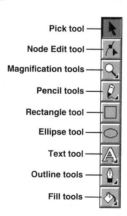

Pick tool

Node Edit tool

Magnification tools

Pencil tools

Rectangle tool

Ellipse tool

Text tool

Outline tools

Fill tools

FIGURE 2.4 The CorelDRAW toolbox

Notice some of your tools have black triangles in the lower-right corner. By clicking on this triangle, you have several options to choose from. For example, the Magnification tool has options to zoom in, zoom out, zoom to actual size, zoom on a selected object, zoom to all objects, and zoom to the full page. We'll cover these extra options in later chapters when we discuss each of the tools in detail.

The Editing Window, Printable Page, and Scroll Bars

The large blank portion of the screen is called the *editing window*. CorelDRAW considers anything in the editing window part of the file. You can place objects anywhere within this window, but you can print only those objects that are contained on the *printable page*, represented by a rectangle. If you want to export the drawing to another format to use it with other software, CorelDRAW exports all your objects, not just what is on the printable page.

The left and right arrows at the bottom of your screen and the up and down arrows at the right-hand edge of your screen are *scroll bars*. They let you view data off the screen when there is more than can fit in the editing window.

Figure 2.5 shows the editing window, the printable page, and the scroll bars.

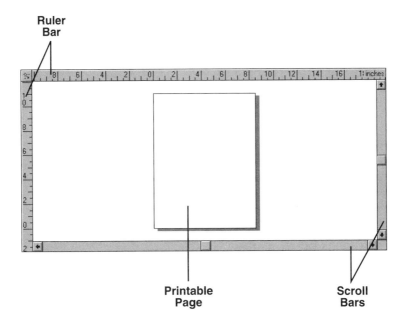

FIGURE 2.5 The editing window, printable page, and scroll bars

The Status Line

On the bottom of the screen is the *status line*, which tells you everything you ever wanted to know about the drawing on which you are currently working. Let's examine it in detail, as illustrated in Figure 2.6.

The numbers in the upper-left corner of the status line indicate the *x* and *y* coordinates of your cursor on the screen.

FIGURE 2.6 *The status line*

The middle of the status line tells you about the type of object selected, as well as its dimensions, the coordinates of its center, how many nodes it has, and what layer it is on. If you are working with text, the middle of the status line also indicates its typeface, font, and point size. The right corner of the status line tells you about the outline and fill of the selected object, including its color and outline width.

You may think that this is fairly obvious information, but as you go on, you'll see that it is easy to lose track of where you are in a drawing that contains many objects.

The Help Pointer

The *Help pointer* is a new feature that helps you identify tools and buttons. If you place your cursor over any screen element, after a moment a yellow box is displayed. It identifies the tool or button you are pointing to. The status line also displays information about the tool or button. Figure 2.7 shows the Help pointer identifying one of the Magnification tool's options.

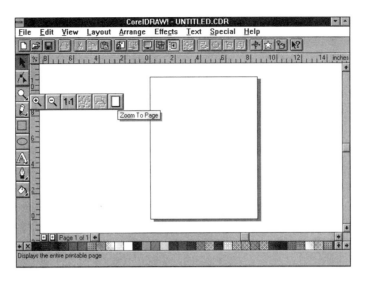

FIGURE 2.7 Using the Help pointer

Summary

You're probably anxious to begin creating graphics with CorelDRAW. This chapter laid the groundwork to do just that. You now know how to launch CorelDRAW, identify the parts of the CorelDRAW screen, recognize the icons in the toolbox, and identify the menu items and their uses.

Chapter 3

Managing Files

This chapter covers the items in the CorelDRAW File menu. Because you put so much work into the drawings that you create, you'll want to save them and work with them again. You may also want to manipulate your CorelDRAW drawings in other software packages or import your files from other software packages to CorelDRAW, as well as print your graphics. This chapter discusses:

❖ Managing files on disk

❖ Setting up a multiple-page file

❖ Importing files

❖ Exporting files

❖ Printing files

Managing Files on Disk

You don't need to remember details about your files when you use CorelDRAW. You can view files easily using either CorelMOSAIC or the Find File feature. CorelDRAW's file management capabilities also include sorting files by name or date saved, annotating or attaching notes to your files, backing up files automatically, and saving files in a format that an earlier version of CorelDRAW can use. To find out more about CorelMOSAIC, refer to *Chapter 10*. To learn more about the rest of CorelDRAW's file management features, read on.

Starting a New File

The **New** option in the File menu clears whatever you are working on from the CorelDRAW screen. If you have a drawing you've modified on the screen and you want to open a new file, CorelDRAW asks you if you first want to save the modified file.

Press **Ctrl-N** to start a new drawing.

SHORTCUT

The **New From Template** option in the File menu allows you to start a new drawing using the styles in a selected template.

When you start a new file, you will usually want to adjust your page settings. To do this, select **Page Setup** from the Layout menu. The Page Setup dialog box is displayed.

This dialog box is set up with tabs, like the tabs on file folders. To select one of the three choices in this dialog box (**Size**, **Layout**, or **Display**), simply click on the corresponding tab to display the appropriate options.

N O T E

❖ **Size**. Click on the drop-down list box to select your paper size. CorelDRAW has 18 page-size options. If none of these sizes suits your needs, choose **Custom** from the pop-up menu to set your own dimensions.

Set the width and height of your page by clicking in the appropriate box or using the increment buttons. Set the measurement unit to inches, millimeters, picas, or points by selecting the option you want from the measurement unit drop-down list.

Click on the **Set From Printer** button to make your page size correspond to the default page size for your printer.

Click on **Portrait** if you want your page to be vertical or tall; click on **Landscape** if you want it to be horizontal or wide.

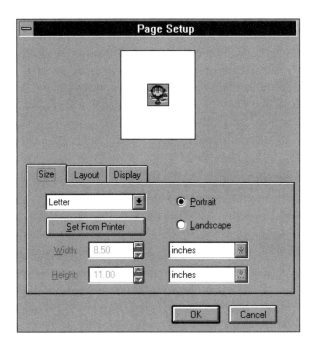

FIGURE 3.1 The Page Setup dialog box with the Size tab selected

❖ **Layout**. The Layout tab automatically sets up your page for a full-page document, a book, a booklet, a tent card, a side-fold card, or a top-fold card. The preview screen at the top of the dialog box demonstrates how each selection works, as shown in Figure 3.2. Figure 3.3 shows each option.

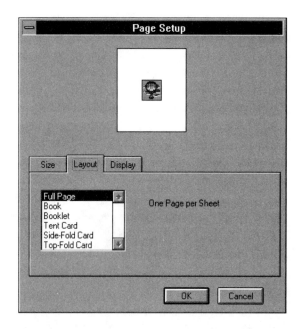

FIGURE 3.2 The Page Setup dialog box with the Layout tab selected

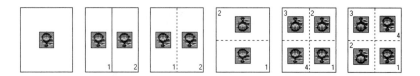

FIGURE 3.3 The layout options, from left to right: full page,
book, booklet, tent card, side-fold card, and top-fold card

❖ **Display**. You can set the Preview screen to match the background of
the paper you want to print on using this option. When you select
Paper Color, a pop-up menu displays giving you several preset colors.
Click on the color you want or select **More** to create new colors. (See
Chapter 7 for more information on using and creating colors.)

N O T E

The color you select does not print. If you want a color background that
prints, select **Add Page Frame**.

Select **Add Page Frame** to place a printable color background on your page. When you select this option it is given the default fill and outline, as with any other object. (See *Chapter 5* for more information on filling and outlining objects.)

Select the **Facing Pages** check box if you are creating a document that has left and right pages. You also have the option of selecting whether the first page is a left page or a right page.

Opening an Existing File

To retrieve a graphics files from the disk, choose **Open** from the File menu.

Press **Ctrl-O** to open a file.

The Open Drawing dialog box, shown in Figure 3.4, lists all the files in the current directory. To choose one, click on its name in the File Name list box. However, if the file you want is not in the current directory, you can choose another directory from the Directories box.

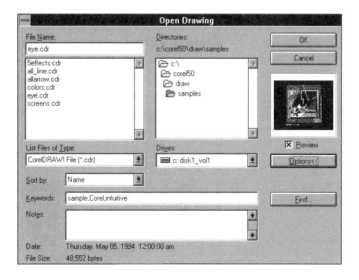

FIGURE 3.4 The Open Drawing dialog box with Preview in effect and Options selected

If you want to see what a file looks like before you open it, click on the file name. If it does not display, click on the **Preview** check box. An image of the file is displayed in the right of the dialog box, as shown in Figure 3.4.

To make it easier to work with your files, you can sort the file names by name or by date.

If the Sort by options are not displayed, click on the Options button to open an extended dialog box.

N O T E

If you have been assigning descriptive keywords to your files, you can also find a file by clicking on **Find** and entering a keyword in the Keyword Search dialog box. If you're looking for a file, and you're not sure where it is, select **Search All Directories** before you do the search.

Saving Your Files

When you select **Save** from the File Menu, the file is automatically saved, with the name appearing on the title bar of the screen. All information about the file, including page size and orientation, print selections, and grid and guideline choices, is saved with the file.

Press **Ctrl-S** to save the file.

SHORTCUT

Whenever you save a file, an automatic backup of the file is created with the .BAK file name extension.

N O T E

To save a file with a new name, choose the **Save As** option from the File Menu, and the Save Drawing dialog box, shown in Figure 3.5, is displayed. Make any changes necessary, including changing the file name or directory in which the file is saved.

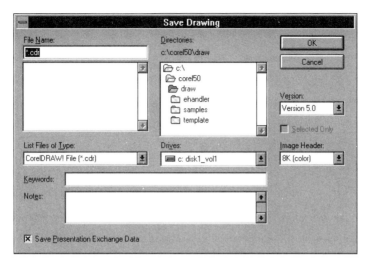

FIGURE 3.5 The Save Drawing dialog box

The Save Drawing dialog box also has options for saving files in earlier CorelDRAW versions (3.0 and 4.0), saving only the selected objects, and saving files with different image headers.

Image headers determine how a file shows up in a preview box. **None** provides no preview, **1K mono** and **2K mono** provide black-and-white previews, and **4K color** and **8K color** provide color previews.

NOTE

If you make extensive changes to a file and still want to retain an original, use the **Save As** option and give the new version another name. You can include keywords or notes about the file to make it easier for you to find and retrieve it the next time you want to open the file. You can also specify an *image header type*, which is a small file with a sketch of your file that allows you to preview the file contents before you retrieve it.

Setting Up a Multiple-Page File

After you add a new page, the number of pages in your document and the currently selected page are indicated on the page counter on the lower-left of your screen, above the status line and color bar.

To add new pages to your document:

1. Select **Insert Page** from the Layout menu or click on the plus sign (+) on the page counter. The Insert Page dialog box, shown in Figure 3.6, is displayed.

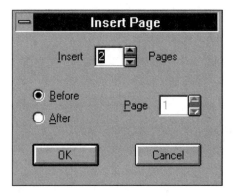

FIGURE 3.6 The Insert Page dialog box

2. Enter the number of pages you want to add or use the increment buttons. Select **Before** to insert the specified number of pages before the current page or select **After** to insert the specified number of pages after the current page.
3. Click on **OK**.

To go to a new page, click on the forward page and previous page arrows on the page counter. You may also select **Go To Page** from the Layout menu and type the page number you want to go to in the dialog box.

If you want to delete pages, select **Delete Page** from the Layout menu. You enter the range of page numbers you want to delete in the Delete Page dialog box.

Importing Files

You can import files of many different formats from a variety of applications into your CorelDRAW graphics files. Refer to the notes in the CorelDRAW reference manual for specific considerations for each file format.

CorelDRAW imports the file formats listed in Table 3.1.

TABLE 3.1 Importing Different File Formats

Application	File Format
Adobe Illustrator	*.AI, *.EPS
AmiPro 2.0, 3.0	*.SAM
ASCII text	*.TXT
AutoCAD DXF	*.DXF
CompuServe bitmap	*.GIF
Computer graphics metafile	*.CGM
Corel Presentation Exchange	*.CMX
CorelCHART	*.CCH
CorelDRAW	*.CDR
CorelPHOTO-PAINT	*.PCX
CorelTRACE	*.EPS
EPS (placeable)	*.EPS, *.PS, *.AI
Excel for Windows 3.0, 4.0	*.XLS
GEM files	*.GEM
HPGL plotter file	*.PLT
IBM PIF	*.PIF
JPEG bitmap	*.JPG, *.JFF, *.JTF
Kodak Photo-CD Image	*.PCD
Lotus 1-2-3 1a, 2.0, 3.0	*.WK?
Lotus PIC	*.PIC
Macintosh PICT	*.PCT
MacWrite II	*.*
Micrographix 2.x, 3.x	*.DRW
Microsoft Rich Text Format	*.RTF
Microsoft Word 5.0, 5.5	*.*
Microsoft Word for Macintosh 4.0, 5.0	*.*
Microsoft Word for Windows 1.x, 2.x, 6.0	*.*, *.DOC
Microsoft Word for Windows 1.x, 2.x, 6.0	*.*, *.DOC
Paintbrush	(*.PCX)
PostScript (interpreted)	*.EPS, *.PS

TABLE 3.1 continued

Rich Text Format	*.RTF
Scitex CT bitmap	*.SCT, *.CT
TARGA bitmap	*.TGA, *.VDA, *.ICB, *.VST
TIFF bitmap	*.TIF, *.SEP, *.CPT
Windows metafile	*.WMF
WordPerfect 5.0, 5.1, 6.0	*.*
WordPerfect Graphic	*.WPG

To import a file:

1. Select **Import** from the File menu.

2. When the Import dialog box is displayed, as shown in Figure 3.7, scroll through the List Files of Type selections and choose the file type you want to import.

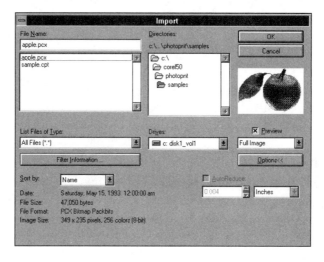

FIGURE 3.7 The Import dialog box with Options selected

3. A list of files with that extension is displayed in the File Name box. If you don't see the file that you want, check that you have the correct drive and directory selected. If you do not, change the drive by clicking on the Drives arrow and selecting a drive from the drop-down list box. Double-click on the correct directory name in the Directories box to select it.

4. When you see the file you need, either double-click on the file name, or click on it once and then click on **OK**. The file is imported and displayed on your screen.

You can import CorelDRAW clip art files from the clip art directories if you've installed them on your hard drive. Clip art directories contain graphics from a wide selection of graphics companies. Once you've imported clip art into your drawing, you can use them as is, or modify them to suit your own needs. Clip art files are stored in *.CDR format. Clip art is covered further in the section on CorelMOSAIC in *Chapter 10*.

Say OLE: Object Linking and Embedding

In the previous section, you learned how to use the **Import** option on the File menu to bring files from other applications into CorelDRAW. Another way to move these files into CorelDRAW is to use *object linking and embedding* (OLE, pronounced *oh-lee*).

When you import a file, the link is *static*. This means that if the imported file needs to be updated, you must leave CorelDRAW, open the file's source application, make your changes, export the file to a format compatible with CorelDRAW, and then repeat the original import function. With OLE, however, you can actively edit the imported file while still in CorelDRAW. OLE is a feature of Microsoft Windows that allows files to be *dynamically linked*.

To insert an object using OLE:

1. Select **Insert Object** from the Edit menu. The Insert Object dialog box is displayed, as shown in Figure 3.8.

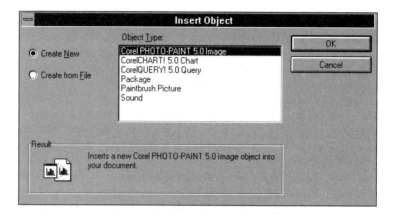

FIGURE 3.8 The Insert Object dialog box

2. To create a source document, choose **Create New**, and then select the source application used to create the object you wish to insert. That application will launch, and you can create the file to be inserted in your document.

NOTE
You may also insert an existing file. Choose **Create From File**, select the source application, and choose the existing file to insert into your document.

3. Click on **OK** to open the source application.

4. When the source application is initiated, create a new file or select an existing one to embed in CorelDRAW.

5. To later edit your embedded file, select the object in your CorelDRAW file and then choose the name of the file from the Object fly-out menu on the Edit menu.

Exporting Files

You may often use CorelDRAW graphics in other applications. For example, you may want to embed a logo in your word processor file. Table 3.2 lists the CorelDRAW file formats.

TABLE 3.2 Exporting to Different File Formats

Application	File Format
Adobe Illustrator	*.AI, *.EPS
Adobe Type 1 font	*.PFB
AutoCAD DXF	*.DXF
CompuServe bitmap	*.GIF
Computer graphics metafile	*.CGM
CorelPHOTO-PAINT	*.PCC
Encapsulated PostScript	*.EPS
GEM files	*.GEM
HPGL plotter file	*.PLT
IBM PIF	*.PIF
JPEG bitmap	*.JPG, *.Jff, *.JTF
Mac PICT	*.PCT
Matrix Imapro SCODL	*.SCD
OS/2 bitmap	*.BMP
TARGA bitmap	*.TGA, *.VDA, *.ICB
TIFF 5.0 bitmap	*.TIF
TIFF 6.0 four-color bitmap	*.SEP
True Type Font	*.TTF
Windows bitmap	*.BMP
Windows metafile	*.WMF
WordPerfect graphic	*.WPG

When you select **Export** from the File menu, the Export dialog box is displayed, as shown in Figure 3.9.

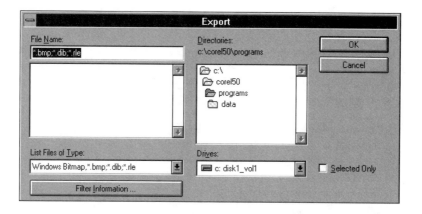

FIGURE 3.9 The Export dialog box

The options in the Export dialog box operate the same way they do in the Import dialog box. An additional feature, however, is the ability to export only selected objects by clicking in the **Selected Only** check box. To do so, you must select the objects you want to export before you choose **Export** from the File menu.

There are special considerations when exporting each type of file. For example, if you are exporting to encapsulated PostScript (*.EPS) format, you'll see the Export EPS dialog box, which lets you select whether all fonts are resident, convert color bitmaps to grayscale, and specify an image header type (and select its resolution).

If you export a bitmap image file, you'll see the Bitmap Export dialog box. This allows you to select the colors, size, resolution, and compression of the exported image.

Printing Files

There are several options and dialog boxes you can use to print from CorelDRAW. This may look like a complicated process, but for the most part, once you establish your print options, they become the default.

To print a file, select **Print** from the File menu. You'll see the basic Print dialog box shown in Figure 3.10.

SHORTCUT

Press **Ctrl-P** to select **Print**.

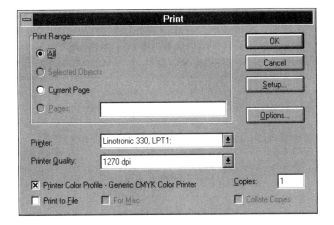

FIGURE 3.10 The Print dialog box

Specifying Print Options

Select **All** to print all pages in your document, **Current Page** to print the page currently shown in your editing window, or **Pages** to select a range of pages. To print only certain objects, select the objects before selecting **Print**. Then, click on the Selected Objects radio button.

From the Printer and Printer Quality drop-down lists, you may select different printers (if you have more than one printer installed), as well as the resolution of your printed document. The Printer Quality value applies to the data sent from CorelDRAW to your printer; to have your output match this value, your printer must also be set to this resolution.

Printer Color Profile enables or disables the color profile selected in CorelDRAW's Color Manager.

Print To File processes your drawing for print and writes it to a disk file. When you select **Print To File** and then select **OK**, a dialog box is displayed. Your disk may now be moved to another computer and spied to the printer. As with the Save As dialog box, you have the opportunity to change the file name or the drive and directory on which the print file is written. You must save these print files with a .PRN file extension, which is automatically inserted for you if you don't specify an extension. Select **For Mac** if the print file will be sent from a Macintosh.

You can also specify the number of copies you want to print. Either type the number of copies you want or click on the scroll arrows to increase or decrease the number. Some basic printers don't allow you to set the number of copies— they print only one copy at a time.

N O T E

It doesn't take twice as long to print two copies as it does to print one. The greatest amount of time is spent in processing your drawing for the printer. Therefore, if you think you'll need multiple copies, you should print them all at once.

It takes time to process a CorelDRAW graphic for print, so be patient. Now may be a good time to take a short break. Of course, the more complex the drawing, the longer it takes. To speed up your printing, you may want to lower the print resolution while you are printing drafts of your graphic, and print it at high resolution only when you are ready for your final copy.

Click on the Options button to access a whole slew of additional print choices. You'll see the Print Options dialog box, which is shown in Figure 3.11.

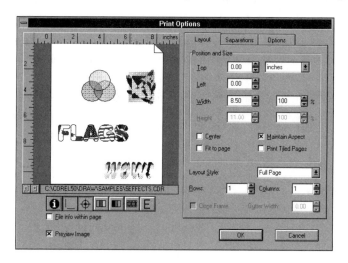

FIGURE 3.11 The Print Options dialog box

Use the button bar to select quickly the following options:

❖ **File Information** places the file name, current date, current time, tile number, and color separation data (if applicable) on the bottom of your page. Normally, this information is placed outside of the active page area. Click on the **File Info Within Page** check box to place this information within the active page area.

❖ **Crop Marks** show the marks delineating the edges of your drawing. To see these marks, the printable page must be smaller than the physical page.

❖ **Registration Marks** show marks to register color for the print. To see these marks, the printable page must be smaller than the physical page.

❖ **Calibration Bar** prints with your drawing calibration bars for each color. These bars allow you to calibrate the colors on your monitor to match exactly the colors on your output.

❖ **Densitometer Scale** causes a printed densitometer to print with your document, showing you the density of your ink for each of the CMYK channels. This display allows for the quality control and consistency of output. This option is available only when you are creating color separations. See *Chapter 7* for a discussion of color and color printing.

❖ **Print Negative** prints the file as a negative (for an imagesetter).

❖ **Emulsion Down** specifies an image with the *emulsion side*—the light-sensitive side of a piece of film—facing down. **Emulsion Up** is the default setting.

You may also select **Preview Image** to view and manipulate your image in the Preview box before printing. You can interactively stretch and scale your image in the Preview box or use the dialog box controls in the **Position** and **Size** portion of the Layout tab. To select a new unit of measurement for your preview, click in the measurement unit box. Your graphic will change accordingly. The bounding box around the previewed graphic indicates the positioning of crop marks.

The Layout Tab

Use the options in the Layout tab, which is shown in Figure 3.12, to adjust how your image is placed on a printed page.

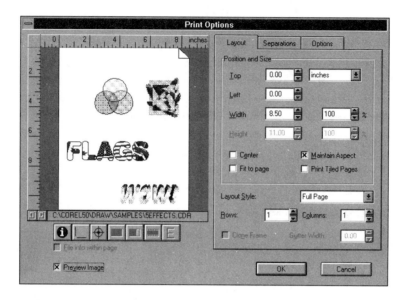

FIGURE 3.12 The Layout tab

❖ **Fit To Page** sizes your graphic to fit on the selected page size. This option allows you to print larger graphics to a smaller size paper or to fit a large graphic on a smaller page.

❖ **Center** centers your graphic on the page as you manipulate it in the Preview window and as you print it.

❖ **Print Tiled Page** prints an oversized drawing on several pages, if necessary.

The Separations Tab

If you are producing color graphics, you must separate your image into the four process colors (CMYK—cyan, magenta, yellow, and black), as well as any custom colors. (See *Chapter 7* for a complete discussion of color.) These options are found in the Separations tab, shown in Figure 3.13.

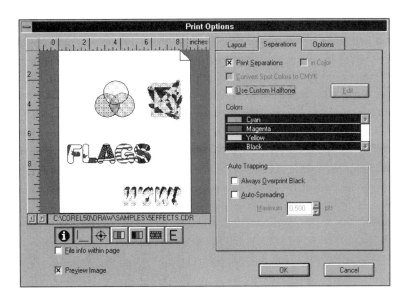

FIGURE 3.13 The Separations tab

Select the Separations check box to enable color separations. **Convert Spot Colors to CMYK** automatically converts any custom colors to CMYK values. **Use Custom Halftone** allows you to create or use custom halftone screens for your images.

Auto Trapping (for PostScript printers only) automatically sets trapping values for your image. *Trapping values* tell your printer how to register and overlap adjoining colors. Consult with your printer or service bureau before adjusting trapping values.

The Options Tab

If you have difficulty printing a file, it may be because you are printing many complex objects that could cause errors in your PostScript printer. It might be a good idea to simplify the curves by reducing the number of segments included in them. Click on the Options tab, shown in Figure 3.14. The normal curve flatness setting is **1**. Increase it to simplify, or flatten, the curves. If you click on the **Auto Increase Flatness** check box, CorelDRAW automatically increases the curve flatness. This either prints the object or, if it is still too complex, causes the printer to skip the object and print the rest of the file.

For a PostScript printer, the **Fountain Steps** option lets you choose the number of stripes that the printer uses to create a fountain fill. A higher number of fountain stripes shows a smoother transition between the different shades but prints more slowly. A lower number results in more visible color bands and faster printing times. You may need to experiment to get an optimum setting.

Reducing the Fountain Steps setting speeds up your print times while you are printing drafts of your objects. Later, you can increase the number when you're ready for the final copy.

N O T E

Summary

The File menu has some very powerful features to manage your CorelDRAW files on disk, to use files from other applications in CorelDRAW, to write your CorelDRAW files on disk in other formats so that you can use them in other applications, and to print your graphics so that you can enjoy the fruits of your labors. We covered several options to help you manage your graphics files, including opening new and existing CorelDRAW files, saving your CorelDRAW files on disk, attaching keyword information to make subsequent retrieval easier, and inserting and manipulating multiple pages in your documents. You also learned how to import files in formats other than CorelDRAW into your graphics files, export your CorelDRAW files to other formats so that you can use them with other applications, and print your CorelDRAW files using print options, printer selection, and page orientation and size.

Chapter 4

Shaping Up:
Using the Drawing Tools

This chapter shows you how to use CorelDRAW's drawing tools to create graphics. It also talks about customizing the CorelDRAW desktop to make it easier for you to create and modify your drawings. Finally, it shows you how to preview your graphics to see how the finished product will look. The topics include:

- ❖ Customizing your desktop
- ❖ Drawing rectangles and squares
- ❖ Drawing ellipses and circles
- ❖ Drawing lines and curves
- ❖ Drawing dimension lines

Customizing Your Desktop

Many creative people who begin working with CorelDRAW can't draw well by hand, and when they first begin working with CorelDRAW, it seems they can't draw well with CorelDRAW either. However, users soon find out that CorelDRAW has some helpful features. For example, displaying rulers and grids makes it easier to align objects on a page and to place objects correctly. CorelDRAW is loaded with features that make precision drawing a snap.

Click on **View** on the menu bar to open the menu shown in Figure 4.1. The View menu customizes your display screen and presents or removes visual aid features. Many of these features are *toggles*, which means they can be turned on or off. For these items, simply click on the feature name. An item is turned on when a check mark appears next to it. A number of helpful items located in the Layout menu are also covered in this section.

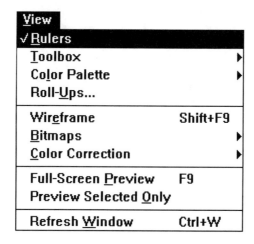

FIGURE 4.1 The View menu

Show Rulers

Because it is often helpful to be able to see the measurements of your page and the objects on it, you'll want to choose the option to see the rulers on your screen. If **Rulers** (the first menu item in the second grouping) is not checked, click on it. Your CorelDRAW desktop is now displayed with the rulers.

Using the Grid

The CorelDRAW grid is another helpful display aid. Along with the rulers, the grid helps you place and space the elements of your drawing. However, unlike the rulers, you need to set up your grid and then display it on the screen. Click on **Grid & Scale Setup** in the Layout menu and a dialog box is displayed, as shown in Figure 4.2.

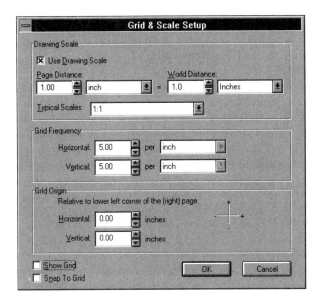

FIGURE 4.2 The Grid & Scale Setup dialog box

Double-click on either the horizontal or vertical ruler to bring up the Grid & Scale Setup dialog box.

SHORTCUT

Use Drawing Scale sets the scale for your artwork. This feature is particularly helpful in preparing architectural plans, industrial drawings, or modeling. For example, you can make a drawing where 1 inch on the page equals a 2-inch actual scale.

The **Grid Frequency** option changes the vertical and horizontal spacing of the grid lines. You can either enter a value or scroll through the numerical values to choose one. You can also change the unit of measurement (inches, millimeters, picas, or points) by scrolling through the choices.

The divisions and units on the ruler reflect the selections you make in the Grid Setup dialog box.

The **Grid Origin** option sets the origin of the grid anywhere in the editing window. The default location is in the lower-left corner of the page. You can also specify the number of grid points per unit as inches, millimeters, picas, or points.

The coordinates you see on the status line reflect the grid origin you entered.

Clicking on **Show Grid** shows the unprintable grid marks on the screen. If you click on the **Snap to Grid** check box, the objects *snap*, or move, to the nearest grid marker whenever you create or move an object. While this feature makes it easier to line up objects, it may also restrict your flexibility. Try it for a while to see if it helps you.

When you're done, click on **OK** to enter your choices and return to the CorelDRAW window.

Guidelines

Guidelines are another form of unprintable line that you can place anywhere on your editing screen. You can place guidelines manually or use specified values in the Guidelines dialog box.

To place guidelines manually:

1. Make sure your rulers are displayed.
2. Click on either of the rulers to display a guideline. Hold down the mouse button while dragging the guideline onto the editing window. Release the mouse when the guideline is in position. Clicking and dragging from the horizontal ruler brings down a horizontal guideline, clicking and dragging from the vertical ruler brings down a vertical guideline.
3. Repeat Step 2 for each guideline you want to place.

To place guidelines using the Guideline dialog box:

1. Select **Guidelines Setup** from the Layout menu to display the Guidelines dialog box, which is shown in Figure 4.3.

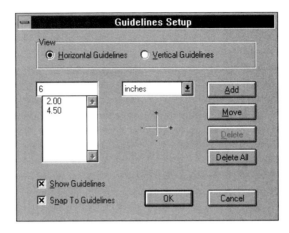

FIGURE 4.3 The Guidelines dialog box

SHORTCUT

Double-click on any existing guideline to display the Guidelines dialog box.

2. Select a **Horizontal** or **Vertical** guideline type from the View field.

3. Enter the desired ruler position or use the increment scroll bars to enter a value.

4. To have items snap to your guideline, make sure **Snap To Guidelines** is checked.

5. Click on **Add** to add your guideline.

6. Repeat Steps 2–5 for each guideline you want to place.

7. Click on **OK** to accept your selections.

Color Palette

As you draw, you'll probably also want to see the color palette at the bottom of your CorelDRAW desktop. When you select **Color Palette** from the View menu, you get a fly-out menu that gives you the following choices:

- ❖ **None**
- ❖ **Uniform Colors**
- ❖ **Custom Colors**
- ❖ **Focaltone Colors**
- ❖ **Pantone Spot Colors**
- ❖ **Pantone Process Colors**
- ❖ **Trumatch Colors**

The selected palette is displayed on the bottom of your screen, just above the status line. Use the scroll arrows on either end of the color bar to scroll through your palette or click on the **Up Arrow** on the right to display the whole palette.

For now, make sure the **Custom Palette** option is selected. For more information on other color palettes, see *Chapter 7*.

Floating Toolbox

The default setting for the position of the toolbox is stationary, or *docked*. To use a floating toolbox that can be positioned anywhere on the screen, select **Floating Toolbox** from the View menu. Your toolbox is now displayed with a docking bar and a title bar, as shown in Figure 4.4.

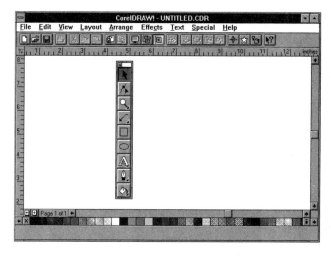

FIGURE 4.4 The floating toolbox

To move your floating toolbox, click on the title bar of the toolbox and drag it into position. To dock your toolbox, double-click on the white bar on the top of the toolbox, or deselect **Floating Toolbox** from the View menu.

On the upper-left of the floating toolbox is a Control-menu bar. Click once on the bar, and the menu shown in Figure 4.5 is displayed.

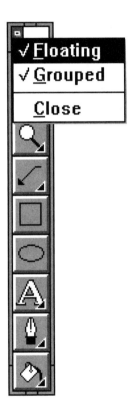

FIGURE 4.5 The Control menu on the floating toolbox

Right now, the **Grouped** option is selected. Deselect this option, and your tools are ungrouped, as shown in Figure 4.6. If you find it cumbersome to work with fly-out menus, this is a great option. The ungrouped toolbox can also be sized like any other window.

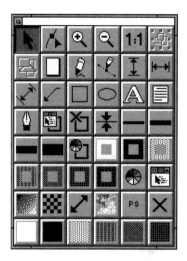

FIGURE 4.6 *The ungrouped toolbox*

By now, you're probably anxious to begin drawing, so let's go.

Drawing Rectangles and Squares

 To draw rectangles and squares, select the Rectangle tool. There are two methods for doing this.

❖ Click on the Rectangle tool in the toolbox.

❖ Press **F6** on your keyboard.

Now that you have selected the Rectangle tool, notice that the Rectangle tool is highlighted and your cursor has changed from an outlined arrow to a cross hair.

To draw a rectangle:

1. Move the cursor to the printable page.

2. Begin drawing your rectangle by holding down the left mouse button and dragging the cursor, as shown in Figure 4.7. An outline shows the position and size of your rectangle as you draw.

3. When the shape is the correct size, release the mouse button.

 Until you release the mouse button, you can keep changing the size and shape of the rectangle by moving your mouse, but you cannot change the starting point.

N O T E

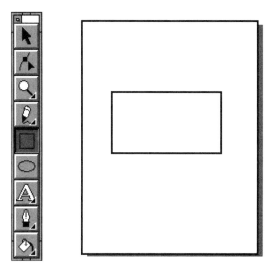

FIGURE 4.7 Drawing rectangles

The Rectangle tool also draws squares. This is done much like drawing a rectangle, but you must hold down the **Ctrl** key while you drag the mouse. The shape is constrained to a square.

 Do not release the **Ctrl** key before you release the mouse button. If you do, the shape will be a rectangle, not a square.

N O T E

When you drew the rectangle and square, you began at one of the outside corners and dragged the mouse to the opposite corner. You can also draw these shapes from the inside out.

To draw a rectangle from the inside out:

1. Move your cursor to the point on the screen where you want the center of the shape to be.
2. While pressing the **Shift** key, click and drag the mouse in either direction. The rectangle forms from the center point that you designated.

You can also draw a square from the center point out by pressing both the **Ctrl** and **Shift** keys while clicking and dragging the mouse.

If you don't like the way your object looks, you can delete it. Select the Pick tool and click on the outline of your object to select it. Your object is selected when eight square handles appear around it. Then, press the **Del** key to erase it.

Drawing Ellipses and Circles

You can draw ellipses and circles the same way you just drew rectangles and squares. Select the Ellipse tool by using one of these two methods.

❖ Click on the Ellipse tool in the toolbox.
❖ Press **F7** on your keyboard.

The Ellipse tool is now highlighted, and the cursor changes from an outlined arrow to a cross hair.

To draw an ellipse:

1. Move the cursor to a place on the printable page where you want to begin drawing your ellipse.
2. Click and drag the cursor in the direction in which you want to draw the ellipse, as shown in Figure 4.8.

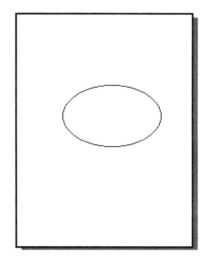

FIGURE 4.8 Drawing an ellipse

3. When the shape is the desired size, release the mouse button.

N O T E

Until you release the mouse button, you can keep changing the size and shape of the ellipse by moving your mouse, but you cannot change the starting point.

To draw a perfect circle, press the **Ctrl** key while you are dragging the mouse. Do not release the **Ctrl** key before you release the mouse button, or your shape will become an ellipse, instead of a circle.

When you drew the ellipse and the circle, you began at one of the outside corners and dragged the mouse to the opposite corner. You can also draw an ellipse from the inside out.

To draw an ellipse from the inside out:

1. Move your cursor to the point on the screen where you want the center of the shape to be.

2. Press the **Shift** key, hold down the mouse button, and drag the cursor so that the ellipse forms on both sides of the center point you designated.

To draw a perfect circle from the inside out, simultaneously press the **Ctrl** and **Shift** keys while clicking and dragging your mouse. You'll see a circle from the center point outward.

You can erase an ellipse or circle by selecting it with the Pick tool and pressing the **Del** key.

Practice Session

Before moving on, draw a few rectangles, squares, ellipses, and circles. This exercise gives you some good practice working with the mouse, as well as with your keyboard. While drawing these shapes, observe a few things:

❖ The status line reflects your current cursor location, as well as the size, shape, and center of your object.

❖ The currently selected object has tiny squares at the corner points if it is a rectangle or square, or on the curve if it is a circle or ellipse. These are *nodes*, which you will use later when you modify, shape, and edit your drawings. They don't appear in your final (or printed) copy.

Drawing Lines and Curves

You would quickly find yourself limited if rectangles and ellipses were the only drawing tools available to you. Fortunately, CorelDRAW provides a Pencil tool for drawing lines and curves.

Drawing Straight Lines

Drawing straight lines is easy with CorelDRAW. Click on the Pencil icon in the toolbox. The Pencil icon becomes highlighted, and the cursor changes from an arrow to a cross hair. Check the status line—you'll see that you're drawing in *Freehand mode*. The Pencil tool also draws in *Bézier mode*. These two methods work in very much the same way when drawing straight lines, but as you'll see, they operate very differently when creating curves. First, let's look at the Freehand mode.

SHORTCUT

Press **F5** to activate the Pencil tool.

Freehand Lines

To draw a straight line in Freehand mode:

1. Position the cursor wherever you want your line to begin; then click and release the mouse button. Be sure to release the mouse button before moving the cursor, or you will draw a curve instead of a straight line.

    Play with your cursor a bit. Watch how easy it is to swing your line upward, downward, or even backward to shorten the line.

2. Move your cursor until the line is at the angle and length that you want.

3. When the line is exactly the way you want it, click the mouse, and a straight line displays as in Figure 4.9. Two small squares at each end of the line designate the node points.

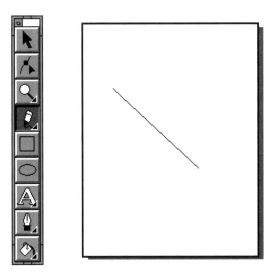

FIGURE 4.9 Drawing in Freehand mode

You can also restrict (or constrain) the angle of your line as you draw. Try doing another line, but this time, constrain the angle of the line to 15°:

1. With the Pencil tool still selected, press the **Ctrl** key before you click the mouse.

2. Hold the **Ctrl** key while you extend the line upward and outward from the starting point.

3. As you move your cursor, notice that the line does not swing freely, but instead, jumps in even increments. These are 15° angles.

4. When the line is where you want it, click the mouse button and then release the **Ctrl** key.

N O T E

If you release the **Ctrl** key before you click the mouse, the line does not remain constrained to the 15° angle.

To practice what you've just learned, keep drawing lines (while holding down the **Ctrl** key) in 15° angles around a center point, until you've drawn a starburst of lines.

Joining Freehand Lines

You can also use the Pencil tool to create a series of joined lines, with each line beginning where the previous line left off. To practice, draw a row of zig-zag lines across the page:

1. Choose a blank spot anywhere on the left side of your page and click the mouse.

2. Choose a point up and to the right and double-click. This location becomes the end point of the first line and the beginning point of the second line.

3. Move the cursor down and to the right and double-click. You ended the second line and started the third.

4. Continue drawing lines in this manner, until you create a zig-zag pattern across the page.

Figure 4.10 illustrates several joined freehand lines.

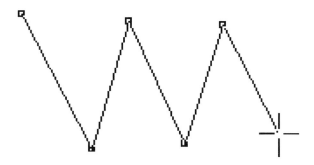

FIGURE 4.10 Several joined freehand lines

Practice Session

Let's get a little more practice with drawing freehand lines before we move on to the next method. Clear the page so that it will be easier to see what you're doing:

1. Open the File menu and click on **New.** Before clearing the screen, CorelDRAW checks to see if you really want to save the current drawing.

2. Click on **No** to clear your editable and printable page.

Now, draw a five-pointed star made of ten lines:

1. Choose a blank spot on your screen and click your mouse to begin.

2. Choose the second point and double-click.

3. Bring the cursor back down and double-click again. The first point of the star is complete.

4. Proceed until you've drawn all five points, as shown in Figure 4.11. You may also want to try this with the **Ctrl** key pressed to constrain the angles.

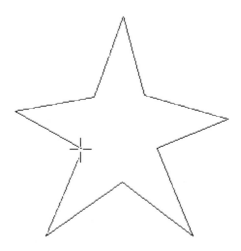

FIGURE 4.11 Drawing a star

If you don't like your star, press **Del** to erase it. If you want to delete only a part of the star, press **Alt-Backspace** (a keyboard shortcut for **Undo**) to wipe out the last segment that you drew.

Bézier Lines

To draw lines in Bézier mode, hold down the mouse button while you click on the black triangle on the lower-right corner of the Pencil tool. You'll see a fly-out menu displaying five icons, as shown in Figure 4.12. The icon on the left that looks like the pencil is for Freehand mode, the next one that looks like a pencil with a dashed line underneath it represents Bézier mode. The remaining three options are for dimension lines and are covered later in this chapter.

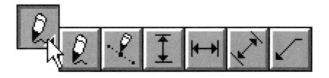

FIGURE 4.12 The drawing mode icons

N O T E

When you select Bézier mode, your toolbox displays the Bézier pencil.

To draw a line in Bézier mode, follow the steps you performed in Freehand mode:

1. Click on a starting point.

2. Move your cursor to the line's ending point.

3. Click the mouse again to complete the line. The status line reminds you that you are in Bézier mode. Also note that when you draw in Bézier mode, the status line indicates that you drew a curve even though you drew a straight line.

Joining Bézier Lines

There's a difference between Freehand and Bézier modes when you draw lines with multiple segments. To see the difference, clear your screen and then do the following:

1. Draw a single line anywhere on the page and single-click at the end of the line.

2. Move your cursor anywhere else on the editable page and click once. A second line is drawn from the end of the first line to the point you just clicked on.

As you can see, there's very little difference between these two methods when drawing straight lines.

Practice Session

For practice, try redrawing the five-pointed star in Bézier mode.

Drawing Curves

Drawing curves is very different in Freehand and Bézier modes, so now is a good time to examine the differences between these two modes.

❖ Freehand curves are drawn along the path you define with your mouse, somewhat like the way you draw curves by hand.

❖ Bézier curves are placed precisely between two defined points (or nodes), resulting in a smoother curve.

Freehand Curves

To draw a freehand curve, make sure your screen is cleared. Check your status line to see if you have selected the Pencil tool and that you are in Freehand mode.

To draw a freehand curve:

1. Move the cursor to a beginning point for your curve and press and hold the mouse button.

2. While holding the mouse button, move the cursor, tracing the path you want the curve to follow, as shown in Figure 4.13.

3. When you are finished drawing your curve, release the mouse button.

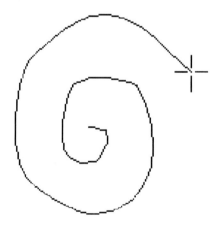

FIGURE 4.13 Drawing a freehand curve

Check the status line and notice that the curve is identified, with the number of nodes in the curve. At the right side of the screen, you'll also see the curve identified as an *open path* (as opposed to a *closed path*, like a rectangle or an ellipse).

To create a *closed curve*, simply make sure that the beginning and end points meet. When you close the curve, the status line no longer shows the figure as an open path.

To erase the entire curve, press either the **Del** key or **Alt-Backspace**. To erase only a portion of the curve while you're drawing it, hold down the **Shift** key while backtracking over the portion of the curve you want to erase.

Just as you drew lines with multiple segments, you can also draw curves with multiple segments using the Pencil tool. To begin a curve with multiple segments:

1. Draw a curve on the screen and release the mouse.

2. Without moving the cursor from the point where you ended the first curve, click the mouse, draw a second curve, and then release the mouse. When you complete the second curve, it will snap to the first, closing any gap between the two, as shown in Figure 4.14.

Your second segment may also be a line.

N O T E

3. Repeat Step 2 for as many segments as you would like to add.

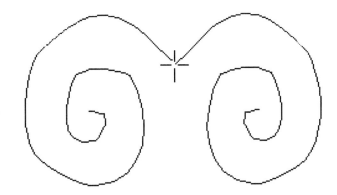

FIGURE 4.14 Drawing multisegment freehand curves

Bézier Curves

Unless you're extremely coordinated (or have done this before), you may be feeling somewhat frustrated, because the curves you drew in Freehand mode have a nursery school quality to them. You can draw curves in Bézier mode more smoothly and precisely, but it may take a little practice.

In Bézier mode, you place a node, specify control points that designate the height and depth of the curve, and then place the next node. Between the two nodes, CorelDRAW places a curve reflecting the control points you specified.

Let's try drawing some curves. First, check your status line to make sure you're in Bézier mode.

1. Select a point somewhere in the middle of your page and then press and release the mouse button. A node (a small filled box) is displayed.

2. Click and hold the mouse button down where you want the curve to end. Drag your mouse until the *control points*, two small boxes connected to the node by a dashed line, are displayed.

3. Drag a control point in the direction that you want the curve to take, as shown in Figure 4.15. Dragging away from the node increases the height and depth. Dragging toward the node decreases the height and depth.

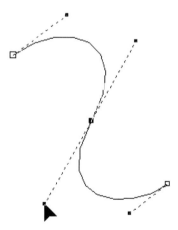

FIGURE 4.15 *Dragging the control points of a Bézier curve*

4. Release the mouse when the curve is the shape you want.

5. Repeat Steps 2 and 3 for each curve segment you want to add.

To change the slope of the curve, rotate the control points around the node.

While you are working on this page, practice drawing other curves. You can make open curves, curves with loops in them, or closed curves. The more you draw different types of curves in Bézier mode, the more skillful you'll become at controlling the curves. As you make your curves, use the grid and rulers. These tools make it easier for you to place the nodes and fix the height and slope of your curves.

AutoJoin

If you need to join lines and curves together, you may want to automatically join, or *autojoin*, them. Using AutoJoin forces two separated nodes of one object to join when they are a specified number of pixels apart. To adjust the AutoJoin parameter, click on the Special menu and select **Preferences**.

Press **Ctrl-J** to open the Preferences dialog box.

Select the Curves tab on the Preferences dialog box, which is shown in Figure 4.16. Click on **AutoJoin** and set the number to **10**.

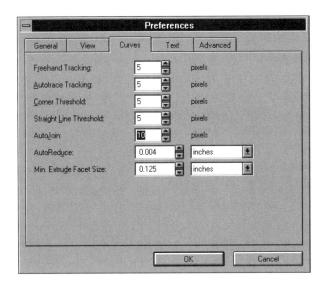

FIGURE 4.16 Setting the AutoJoin parameters in the Curve tab of the Preferences dialog box

Using AutoJoin forces two separated end nodes of one object to join when they are at most 10 pixels apart. The default setting is 5. A lower AutoJoin number prevents nodes from automatically joining unless you draw them precisely—a larger number is more forgiving.

Drawing Dimension Lines

Dimension lines are commonly used in technical drawings to illustrate the dimensions of objects or the distance between them. There are four dimension tools in the Pencil tool fly-out menu: vertical, horizontal, angled, and callout. They are shown in Figure 4.17.

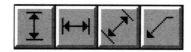

FIGURE 4.17 *The vertical, horizontal, angled, and callout dimension drawing tools*

To draw a dimension line:

1. Select the Dimension Vertical tool.

2. Click on the point where you want to begin measuring and hold down the mouse button.

3. Drag the dimension line toward the point where you want to stop measuring.

4. Double-click on the ending point.

N O T E

The measurement of the dimension line is displayed as text between the ends of the dimension line and is expressed in the same units you selected for your rulers. You may need to use the Zoom tool on the line to see the measurement.

The Dimension Callout tool provides an incredibly easy method for annotating drawings.

1. Select the Dimension Callout tool.

2. Click on the area you want to annotate and then double-click where you want to place your text. Type in your text, as shown in Figure 4.18.

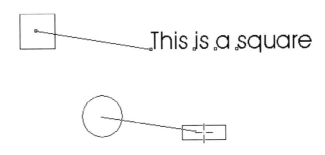

FIGURE 4.18 Using the Dimension Callout tool to annotate a drawing

You can change your measurement and callout text as you would any other text object. Please refer to *Chapter 6* for more details on formatting text.

Summary

You now know how to customize your desktop; how to draw circles, ellipses, rectangle, and squares; and how to draw freehand and Bézier lines and curves. You also learned how to draw dimension lines and how to create callouts.

Chapter 5

Manipulating Objects

Graphics would be pretty boring if they were only simple line drawings. So this chapter covers:

- ❖ Moving and modifying objects
- ❖ Previewing your drawing
- ❖ Filling and outlining objects
- ❖ Shaping objects
- ❖ Arranging objects

Moving and Modifying Objects

 The Pick tool, the arrow icon at the top of the toolbox, is very powerful. When you select this tool, you can move, size, scale, and rotate any object on your screen.

Before using this tool, let's create a page to work with. Clear the current screen and draw these objects: a rectangle, a circle, a line, and a curve.

Moving Objects

Follow these steps to move an object:

1. Click on the Pick tool.

 Press the **Spacebar** to select the Pick tool after creating any object except text.

SHORTCUT

2. Move your cursor to a point on the rectangle you drew on your page and click the mouse button to select it. Rectangular handles are displayed.

3. Drag the rectangle anywhere on the page, using one of the four corner nodes. A dashed rectangle shows the new location.

4. When you are satisfied with the new location, release the mouse button, and your rectangle is displayed in its new location (see Figure 5.1). Click again to de-select the rectangle.

FIGURE 5.1 Moving objects

You should practice moving the different objects around the page until you're confident you can place them exactly in their new locations.

You can also select **Transform** roll-up from the Effects menu to move your objects. You may want to use this option to move an object if you know exactly where you want the object to go, or if you want to move the object a specific distance from its present location.

1. Select the object you want to move and click on **Transform** in the Arrange menu to open the Transform roll-up menu. Select the top left icon, which selects Move mode.

N O T E

A *roll-up menu* is a dialog box that remains on the screen all of the time but that can be rolled up to keep your screen uncluttered. There's an up arrow in the upper-right corner of the menu and a control menu in the upper-left corner. Once you've accessed and used a roll-up menu, simply click on the up arrow to roll it up and out of the way, much the same way as you would roll up a window shade. The title bar remains visible. When you need the dialog box again, click on the down arrow (on the right), and the roll-up menu is restored. In every roll-up menu, simply select your settings and then click on **Apply** to accept them.

SHORTCUT

Press **Alt-F7** to open the Transform roll-up menu in Move mode (see Figure 5.2).

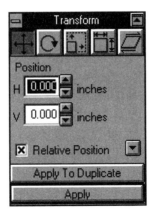

FIGURE 5.2 The Transform roll-up menu in Move mode

2. In the roll-up menu, enter the distance you want to move the object in the Horizontal and Vertical fields.

Reshaping Objects

The Pick tool also lets you reshape objects. With the Pick tool selected, click on any outer edge of an object. You'll see the eight small black boxes, called *handles*, displayed around the object. Use these handles to stretch, shrink, or scale an object.

Stretching Objects

To stretch the rectangle horizontally:

1. Select the rectangle on your page.
2. Move your cursor over one of the handles on the vertical edge of the rectangle until the cursor becomes a cross hair.
3. Click and hold the mouse button. When the dotted rectangle appears, drag outward with your mouse. Watch the side of the rectangle that you selected stretch outward, as shown in Figure 5.3.

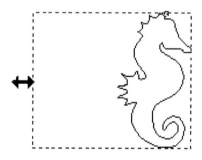

FIGURE 5.3 Stretching an object

Sizing Objects

You can also shrink or enlarge an object in much the same way:

1. With the rectangle still selected, move the cursor over one of the handles on the horizontal edge of the rectangle until it becomes a cross hair.

2. Click and hold the mouse button.

3. When the dotted rectangle appears, drag inward. The side of the rectangle you selected shrinks inward.

So far you've used the Pick tool to resize the object, but it was not resized *proportionally*—the rectangle no longer has the same proportions as it did when you first drew it. To resize proportionally:

1. Click on the rectangle.

2. When the handles appear, move your cursor to one of the corner handles until it becomes a cross hair.

3. Press and hold the mouse button, and the dotted rectangle is displayed.

4. As you drag outward, the rectangle stretches slowly in the direction you move the mouse. A dotted rectangle is displayed as you stretch the object. The rectangle is being stretched in increments that maintain its *proportions*, the ratio of width to height.

While you are stretching, shrinking, or scaling an object, you can create a copy of the original object.

1. Select the curve that you drew and select one of the handles with your cursor.

2. Stretch the object while simultaneously holding down the + (plus sign) key on the numeric keyboard.

3. When you're done, release both the mouse button and the + key. You'll see your stretched object as well as a copy of the original object.

Sizing can also be accomplished through the Transform roll-up menu. Select the fourth icon on the top row to engage Sizing mode (see Figure 5.4).

SHORTCUT

Press **Alt-F11** to switch to Sizing mode.

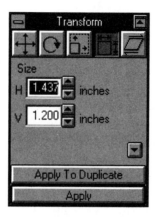

FIGURE 5.4 The Transform roll-up menu in Sizing mode

Rotating, Skewing, and Mirroring Objects

You can also use the Pick tool to rotate, skew, or mirror an object.

Rotating Objects

Follow these steps to rotate an object:

1. Move your cursor to the rectangle on your page and double-click on any edge of the object. You'll see a series of double-headed arrows appear around the rectangle.

2. Move the cursor to one of the curved double arrows in a corner until the cursor becomes a cross hair.

3. Press and hold the mouse button, and the dotted rectangle is displayed.

4. Drag it in the direction you want to rotate the rectangle. Your cursor becomes a small horseshoe shape with an arrow on each end.

5. When you've rotated the rectangle to the location and in the direction that you want, release the mouse button (see Figure 5.5).

FIGURE 5.5 Rotating an object

While you are rotating an object, you can control, or *constrain*, the angle of rotation. Hold the **Ctrl** key while dragging the object, and the object rotates in increments of 15°.

If you press the **+** key on the numeric keypad while rotating the object, a copy of the original remains on the screen.

To rotate objects more precisely, select the second icon on the Transform roll-up menu to enter Rotation mode. Enter values for the angle and center of rotation and then click on **Apply**.

Press **Alt-F8** to switch to Rotation mode (see Figure 5.6).

SHORTCUT

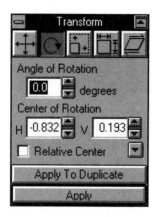

FIGURE 5.6 The Transform roll-up menu in Rotation mode

Skewing Objects

When the double-headed arrows are around your object, you can also skew it. Unlike rotating, which maintains the same shape but simply turns it around, skewing pulls the object in a direction, slanting it either horizontally or vertically.

Follow these steps to skew an object:

1. Move the cursor over the side handles until it changes to a cross hair.

2. Drag the object in the direction you want to skew it. The dotted box skews as you drag the cursor.

3. When the dotted outline is the shape you want, release the mouse button.

While rotating or skewing an object, use the **Ctrl** key to constrain the amount of rotation. Don't forget that using the **+** key leaves the original behind as before.

To skew objects more precisely, select the last icon on the Transform roll-up menu to enter Skew mode (see Figure 5.7). Enter values for the horizontal and vertical skew and then click on **Apply**.

SHORTCUT

Press **Alt-F12** to switch to Skew mode.

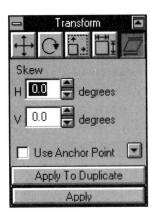

FIGURE 5.7 The Transform roll-up menu in Skew mode

Mirroring Objects

You can also flip an object to create a mirror image of that object:

1. Select one of the objects that you just rotated.

2. Drag one of the side handles back across the object while holding the **Ctrl** key, and a mirror image of the object is displayed.

The **Ctrl** key constrains the image to increments of 100% of its original size while mirroring. Without the **Ctrl** key, your image is not truly mirrored, because it will be a different size than the original. You also can mirror an object while leaving the original by pressing the **+** key on the numeric keyboard while dragging back across the object.

To mirror vertically, select the top or bottom middle handle and drag the handle through the object.

You can also stretch an object by using the Transform roll-up menu. Click on the center icon, which is the scale and mirror option.

SHORTCUT

Press **Alt-F9** to open the Transform roll-up menu in Scale and Mirror mode. If the Transform roll-up is already open, pressing **Alt-F9** switches to Scale and Mirror mode for you (see Figure 5.8).

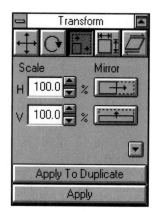

FIGURE 5.8 The Transform roll-up menu in Scale and Mirror mode

Enter the percentage you want to stretch the object, vertically and/or horizontally. For example, if you enter **50%** in the Horizontal box and **0%** in the Vertical box, the image will be half as wide, but the same height. You can choose to mirror the object either horizontally or vertically.

Click on the horizontal or vertical mirror buttons or select both. When you are ready to accept your settings, click on **Apply**.

Undo, Redo, Delete, Duplicate, and Clone

There are several handy options on the Edit menu that can help you manage the objects on your screen.

Undo

If you select **Undo** from the Edit menu, CorelDRAW undoes the last command or action that you performed. In other words, if you moved, stretched, scaled, or rotated an object, and you don't like the results of the last action, select **Undo**.

Press **Ctrl-Z** or **Alt-Backspace** to undo a previous action or command.

SHORTCUT

Redo

If you change your mind again, select **Redo** from the Edit menu, and CorelDRAW redoes the previous action or command.

Delete

You can select the **Delete** option from the Edit menu to erase an object from your screen as an alternative to pressing the **Del** key.

Duplicate

You can use the Edit menu to create a duplicate of an object on the screen. With an object selected, select **Duplicate** from the Edit menu, and a duplicate of the object is displayed. The duplicate is placed in a location defined in Preferences in the Special menu.

Press **Ctrl-D** to create a duplicate of the object.

SHORTCUT

Clone

Cloning and duplicating are different functions. *Duplicating* creates an independent replica of your object, while *cloning* creates a new object that automatically assumes the changes applied to the original, or master, object. For example, if you change the outline and fill of the master object, the outline and fill of the clone are changed as well.

If you select a clone and perform an operation on it, the attribute you change will no longer be attached to the master. For example, if you select a clone and change its outline, then any subsequent changes made to the outline of the master will no longer apply to the clone.

First create the clone by selecting **Clone** from the Edit menu. Using the right mouse button, click on a master object. The Object menu is displayed and provides options for selecting the master's clones. If you click on a clone with the right mouse button, the Object menu displays an option to select a master.

Practice Session

You know enough of the basics of CorelDRAW to create a simple drawing. Before you begin drawing, clear your page.

This drawing is the beginning of a simple beach poster. First, let's draw a beach chair on the left side of the page.

1. Select the Rectangle tool and, halfway down the left side of the page, draw a horizontal rectangle. This forms the back of your director's chair.

2. About 1.5 inches down, draw a narrow horizontal rectangle, of the same width; then connect the two rectangles with a line on either side.

3. Put some legs on the chair. Select the Ellipse tool. Starting at the bottom of the lower rectangle, draw a narrow ellipse (see Figure 5.9).

4. Press the **Spacebar** to select the Pick tool. (The ellipse will still be selected.) Double-click on the node until the rotate arrows appear; then rotate the ellipse until it is in a diagonal position.

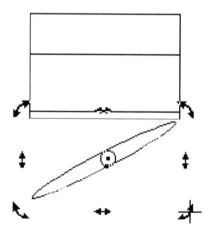

FIGURE 5.9 *The beach chair takes shape*

5. Create a duplicate mirror image of the narrow ellipse. While holding the + key on the numeric keypad, drag one of the side handles of the ellipse

back over the ellipse. You'll see a mirrored duplicate of the ellipse. Move the two ellipses until they form the crossed legs of the director's chair. Congratulations! You've created your first graphic (see Figure 5.10).

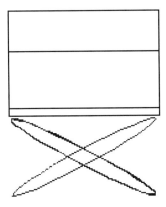

FIGIURE 5.10 Your first graphic—a beach chair

6. Before we continue our beach poster, save what you've done so far. From the File menu, select **Save**. The Save Drawing dialog box is displayed.

7. Be sure you have selected the directory in which you want to save your drawing. In the File Name box, enter the file name **BEACH**.

All CorelDRAW files automatically have the standard *.CDR file extension attached.

N O T E

8. Click on **OK.** CorelDRAW returns to the drawing page. Note that an hourglass appears while the file is being written to disk.

9. To continue drawing the poster, add a beach ball in the extreme lower-right corner of the page. Select the Ellipse tool, and while you drag with your mouse, hold the **Ctrl** key to form a circle (see Figure 5.11).

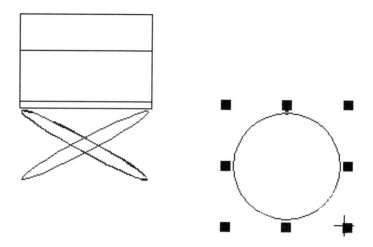

FIGURE 5.11 *The outline of a beach ball*

10. Finish the beach ball by selecting the Pencil tool and adding some curves (see Figure 5.12). You can do these in either Freehand or Bézier mode, but you'll have more control over your lines if you use Bézier mode.

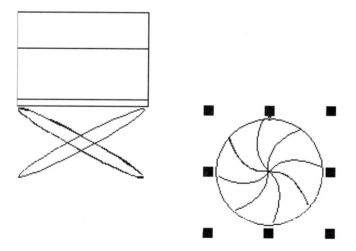

FIGURE 5.12 *The completed beach ball*

11. To complete our poster (at least for the time being), let's tie a kite to the chair. Select the Rectangle tool and, in the upper-right corner, draw a rectangle. Rotate it, skew it, and then stretch it, until it forms a diamond shape (see Figure 5.13).

12. With the Pencil tool selected, add horizontal and diagonal lines across the body of the kite.

13. Create a curve to "tie" the kite to the arm of the director's chair.

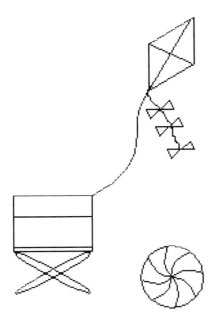

FIGURE 5.13 The beach poster with a kite

Later, we'll work with the Outline and Fill tools to spruce up our poster. In the meantime, though, let's save our file. From the File menu, select **Save**, and the file is automatically saved on disk, with the name that you assigned before.

Previewing Your Drawing

You have three viewing options in CorelDRAW: the wireframe, editable preview, and full-screen preview.

Wireframe is the mode you have worked with so far. It simply shows a thin outline of your graphic, not any applied outlines or fills. The *Editable preview* displays outlines and fills while allowing you to manipulate your drawings. The *full-screen preview* displays your graphic across the entire screen.

SHORTCUT

Press **Shift-F9** to toggle between the wireframe and editable preview.

Use a full-screen preview to see what this practice page looks like. Open the View menu and select **Full Screen Preview**. Pressing **F9** also gives you a full-screen preview. Pressing **F9** again returns your screen to the format you previously had, either the wireframe or the editable preview.

You may also select **Preview Selected Only** from the View menu to show only the currently selected object in a preview. If you are working on a complex drawing that takes a while to redraw itself, this is a time-saving option.

Filling and Outlining Objects

CorelDRAW provides a number of fill and outline tools. These include textured, PostScript, and colored fill patterns and a large selection of dotted lines and arrowheads.

The Fill Tool

The Fill tool is displayed on your tool box as a bucket of paint. To fill an object and select the object, and then click on the Fill tool. A fly-out menu showing the various fill options is displayed (see Figure 5.14).

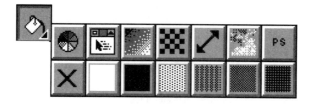

FIGURE 5.14 The Fill tool fly-out menu

Let's define the items on the fly-out menu (from left to right, top to bottom).

❖ **Uniform Color Fill**, represented by a color wheel, selects a solid color to fill your object.

❖ **Fill Roll-Up**, represented by a small menu, activates the Fill roll-up menu (see Figure 5.15), which contains many of the options from the Fill tool fly-out menu.

FIGURE 5.15 The Fill roll-up menu

❖ **Fountain Fill**, represented by a shaded color blend from one color to another, is available by selecting the shaded box.

❖ **Two-Color Fill**, represented by a checkerboard square, to fill your object with a two-color pattern.

❖ **Full-Color Fill**, represented by a diagonal, double-headed arrow, allows you to access full-color patterns and select one to fill your object.

❖ **Bitmap Texture Fill**, represented by clouds, provides over 100 different bitmap textures.

❖ **PostScript Fill**, represented by the letters *PS*, selects PostScript effects, if you are using a PostScript printer.

❖ **No Fill**, represented by an *X*, creates a transparent object with no fill. If there are other objects under an unfilled object, they show through.

❖ **Shades of Gray** (white, black, and four shades of gray) are available from the bottom row of the Fill tool fly-out menu.

You can fill only closed objects. An open path must be closed before you can fill it.

N O T E

Color Fill

Let's start by choosing some uniform color fill for our beach ball. Make sure that the beach ball is selected; then, click on the color wheel. The Uniform Fill dialog box, which is shown in Figure 5.16, is displayed.

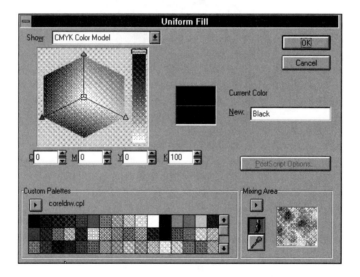

FIGURE 5.16 The Uniform Fill dialog box

If you do not have any objects selected, the Uniform Fill for New Object dialog box is displayed. This dialog box sets the defaults for objects being created. You can click on any of the three options shown and then click on **OK** to confirm or **Cancel**, which allows you to return to the page and click on the correct object.

N O T E

Choose a bright red from the palette: Click on the color, and the beach ball will be filled in. Choose another color and fill in the kite.

You can create your own colors by "mixing" the process inks—cyan, magenta, yellow, and black. There are many guide wheels and books available to help you determine what percentages of these inks create the colors you want.

Two-Color Patterns

To fill your object with a two-color pattern, select the Two-Color Fill icon (checkerboard square) from the Fill tool fly-out menu. The Two-Color Pattern dialog box is displayed, as shown in Figure 5.17.

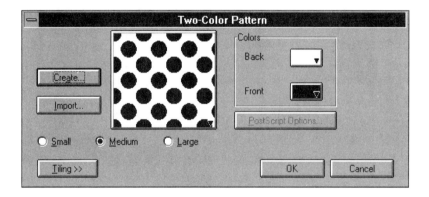

FIGURE 5.17 The Two-Color Pattern dialog box

To view all of the patterns, click on the pattern preview box. Scroll through the patterns on the fly-out menu until you find one you like and then select **OK** or double-click on your selection.

The **Back** and **Front** options change the background and foreground colors. As you change the selections, you'll see the pattern preview box change.

Patterns are made up of tiles, and you can stagger them in the same way that you arrange tiles on a floor or a wall. CorelDRAW lets you change the way the individual tiles in your pattern repeat.

Click on **Tiling** in the Two-Color Pattern dialog box, and you'll see an extended and detailed dialog box. Select **Create** to make your own patterns. Changing the first tile offset shifts the entire pattern either horizontally or vertically. The **Row/Column** option changes the offset within an individual repetition.

You can also access two-color patterns through the Fill roll-up menu. Click on the small menu icon, then on the checkerboard icon on the roll-up menu. Click on the arrow in the pattern preview box to see the fly-out selection menu, which is shown in Figure 5.18. Select a pattern as you did in the Two-Color Pattern dialog box.

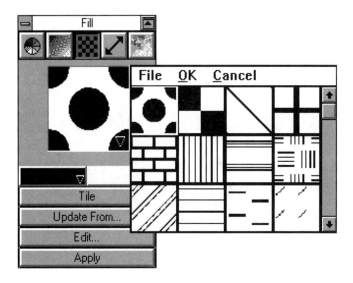

FIGURE 5.18 Choosing a two-color pattern from the Fill roll-up menu

You can choose small, medium, and large versions of your pattern. Change the size of the small, medium, and large tiles by clicking on **Tiling** and then filling in using the height and width boxes.

Click on **Tile** on the Fill roll-up menu, and a node is displayed allowing you to shape and stretch a tile shape manually. Click on **Apply** to see the new tiling effect.

Go back to your beach drawing and choose a tiled two-color pattern for the back of the director's chair.

Full-Color Patterns

The full-color pattern option, accessible from the Fill tool fly-out menu or the Fill roll-up menu, works in much the same way as the two-color pattern. Full-color patterns, which are shown in Figure 5.19, are vector graphics.

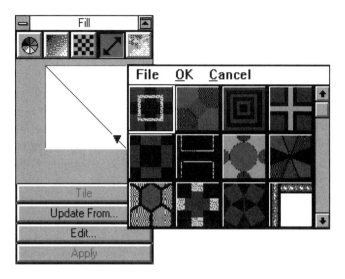

FIGURE 5.19 Some full-color pattern choices

Fountain Fill

A *fountain fill* is a blend or tint from one color to another that gives a shaded effect. Select a fountain fill from the Fill fly-out menu or the Fill tool roll-up menu.

The fountain fill shown in the preview box of Figure 5.20 has a *linear fill*, which means that the fill occurs in a particular direction that you specify.

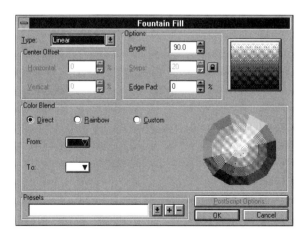

FIGURE 5.20 The Fountain Fill dialog box

A *radial fill* radiates from the center outward. You can move the center point to create a point of light by specifying a percentage in the Center Offset field.

You can change the colors of the fountain fill by clicking on the **Custom** box in the Color Blend portion of the dialog box.

Change the beach ball to a radial fountain fill to give it a feeling of depth. If you have a PostScript printer, you can click on **PostScript Options** and choose from a variety of available halftone screens.

Bitmap Texture Fill

In addition to bitmap patterns, you can fill your object with a bitmap texture. Over 100 different textures are available in the Texture Fill dialog box (see Figure 5.21) including clouds, fiber, flames, gravel, paper textures, and watercolor. Texture fills are available from both the Fill tool fly-out menu and the Fill roll-up menu.

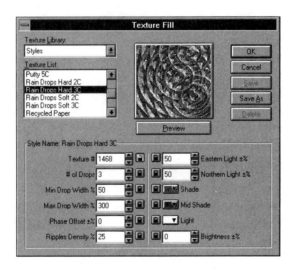

FIGURE 5.21 The Texture Fill dialog box

PostScript Textures

If you are a PostScript printer user, you can also choose from a list of PostScript textures (an earlier version of patterns) (see Figure 5.22). These patterns appear in printed pieces, but not on the screen. On the screen, objects fill with the letters *PS*. Samples of these textures are available in your CorelDRAW documentation.

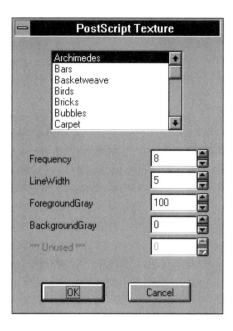

FIGURE 5.22 The PostScript Texture dialog box

Black-and-White Fill

If you are drawing or printing in simple black and white, use the bottom row of fill patterns on the Fill tool fly-out menu. You can choose black, white, and four shades of gray for your graphics.

Let's continue working on the beach graphic you have been drawing. Choose a medium-gray fill for the legs of the director's chair. Then, save your drawing by selecting **Save** from the File menu.

The Outline Pen Tool

 The Outline Pen tool is displayed on your tool box as a pen point. To change an outline, select the object and then click on the Outline Pen tool. A fly-out menu showing the various outline options is displayed, as shown in Figure 5.23.

Press **F12** to select the Outline Pen dialog box.

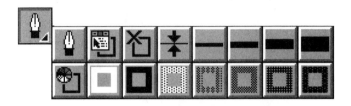

FIGURE 5.23 The Outline Pen fly-out menu

Select the Pen icon from the fly-out menu to choose the default outline style for your objects. If no object is currently selected, a dialog box, which lets you to select new defaults, is displayed .

The next item on the fly-out menu is the small menu icon. Clicking on this icon activates the Pen roll-up menu, which is shown in Figure 5.24.

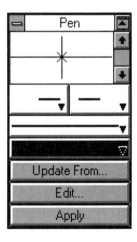

FIGURE 5.24 The Pen roll-up menu

Just as with the Fill roll-up menu, you can make many of your outline selections from the Pen roll-up menu.

Outline Width

The remainder of the selections on the top row of the Outline Pen fly-out menu allow you to choose the outline thickness, including *X* for no outline. You may want to experiment with these thicknesses to select the outline size you would like to have for your object. You can also choose a shade of gray or a color for your outline using the options on the bottom row of the Outline Pen fly-out menu.

To continue enhancing the beach drawing, choose a wide outline and draw two supports for the director's chair that connect the back to the seat.

You can make several selections from the Outline Pen dialog box:

❖ **Color**. Clicking on the arrow displays the list of colors you can use for the outline's color.

❖ **Width**. You can enter the width and the unit of measurement you would like to apply to the outline.

❖ **Corners** and **Line Caps**. Here you can select the corner and line cap styles for your outlines. Beside each check box, the option is visually shown.

❖ **Behind Fill**. You can also place your outlines behind the fill of an object, using the check box at the bottom of the screen. Placing the outline behind the fill makes the outline appear thinner.

❖ **Scale With Image**. Selecting this check box at the bottom of the screen scales the outline with an object, which changes the outline's thickness. For example, if you enlarge an object, the outline also becomes thicker.

❖ **Arrows**. This is one of the more powerful outline tools, and it allows you to choose a type of line ending. At the upper-right corner of the dialog box (and on the Pen roll-up menu) are two arrow preview boxes. Click on the line end you want to select (beginning or end), and a selection of arrowheads is displayed, as shown in Figure 5.25.

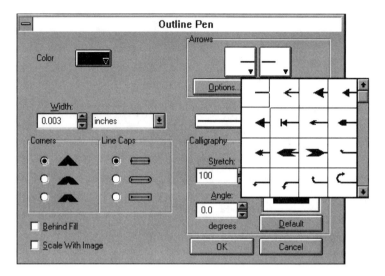

FIGURE 5.25 Arrowhead selection

Make a selection, and the preview box reflects your choice. If you do not see the arrowhead you want, tailor an existing one to your needs. Select **Options** and then select **Edit**. Using the Arrowhead Editor, you can perform some basic editing on an arrowhead.

❖ **Line Styles**. Click on the line preview box under style, and a variety of choices, including dotted and dashed lines, is displayed.

❖ **Calligraphy**. You can create a calligraphic outline by changing the stretch, angle, and rotation of the pen nib.

Shaping Objects

CorelDRAW places nodes on objects, as we saw when we drew lines and curves in *Chapter 4*. These nodes are used to change the shape of objects.

Shaping Rectangles and Ellipses

The easiest shaping tasks you can perform in CorelDRAW are shaping rectangles and ellipses. So, before we begin learning about the Shape tool, draw a few rectangles and ellipses on the screen.

Shaping Rectangles

To begin, let's click on the Shape tool. The cursor changes from a cross hair to a filled arrowhead. Use this cursor to select one of the rectangles on your screen.

Notice that your rectangle has a node in each corner. Select a node and drag it down and around the corner (see Figure 5.26).

N O T E

When you click on a node, it changes from a hollow box to a filled box. When you drag the node, the corners of the rectangle become rounded. The corners of the rectangle have now been changed to curves.

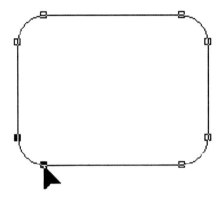

FIGURE 5.26 Dragging a node of a rectangle with the Shape tool

If, later on, you choose the Pick tool to stretch, shrink, or skew a rectangle you've already shaped, the curved corners of the rectangle stretch, shrink, or skew along with the rest of the rectangle.

Shaping Ellipses

The Shape tool can create arcs or pie wedges from ellipses and circles. Select the Shape tool and use the shape cursor (the black arrowhead) to select an ellipse. Place the arrowhead on the ellipse's single node.

To create an arc from the ellipse, click and drag the mouse in a circle with the cursor outside the ellipse. As you drag the mouse, you'll see the node split in two. When the arc is the length that you want, release the mouse button (see Figure 5.27).

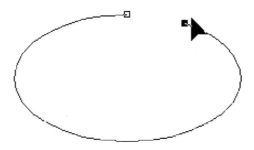

FIGURE 5.27 Dragging the node of an ellipse with the Shape tool

The status line shows the location of the two new nodes, as well as the angle created between them.

You can create a wedge from the ellipse by selecting the Shape tool and then selecting another ellipse or circle to shape. Again, click on the single node and then click and drag the mouse. However, instead of dragging along the outside of the outline, you drag the node with the cursor inside the ellipse or circle, as shown in Figure 5.28.

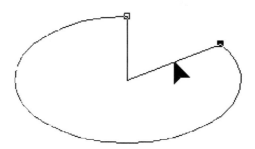

FIGURE 5.28 Using the Shape tool to make a wedge

Again, the status line shows the location of the two new nodes, as well as the angle between the nodes.

The Zoom Tool

Sometimes when you are working on an object, you might find it difficult to see clearly the section you want to change. Particularly when you're using the Shape tool to work with curves with multiple nodes, you may need a close-up view of one or two of the nodes. To help you focus on what you need to see (or to expand it to get the big picture), CorelDRAW has a Zoom tool, the third item on the toolbox.

When you click on the Zoom tool, a fly-out menu offers five options, as shown in Figure 5.29.

FIGURE 5.29 The Zoom tool fly-out menu

Zoom In

 The first tool, Zoom In, displays a magnifying glass with the plus sign. When you select the Zoom In icon, the cursor becomes a magnifying glass. Click and drag the mouse over the portion of the page you want to magnify.

 Press **F2** to select the zoom In option.

If you think you'll need to zoom in frequently, you can program your right mouse button to zoom in. From the Special menu, choose **Preferences**. From the General tab, shown in Figure 5.30, select the action you want for the right mouse button. In this case, you would select **.2X Zoom** and then click on **OK**.

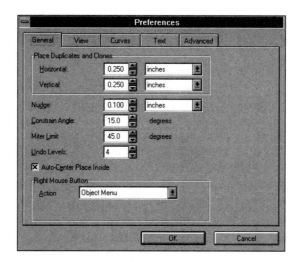

FIGURE 5.30 The Preferences dialog box

There are several options for programming the right mouse button. Select the feature you think you'll use most often, click on its check box, and click on **OK**.

N O T E

Remember that while using the Zoom In tool, you still have access to your entire graphic. Use the scroll bars at the top and sides of your screen to move the drawing in the window.

Zoom Out

You can use the Zoom Out tool, shown as a magnifying glass with a minus sign, to reduce the magnification to the previous zoom level.

Press **F3** to zoom out one magnification level. Remember, however, that you can keep zooming out until your page is smaller than the original.

SHORTCUT

Actual Size

The third tool, 1:1, displays the objects on your screen as close as possible to the size they will appear on the printed page.

Zoom to Selected

The Zoom to Selected tool zooms in on the currently selected item. If no object is selected, this option is grayed out.

All Objects

The All Objects tool changes the magnification so that everything you've drawn, whether or not it fits on the printable page, is displayed. If there is nothing on your page, this option is grayed out.

Zoom to Page

The Zoom to Page tool changes the magnification so that the entire printable page is displayed.

Press **F4** to execute the Zoom to Page tool.

Shaping Lines and Curves

Shaping lines and curves is more involved than shaping ellipses or rectangles because:

❖ Lines and curves have multiple nodes.

❖ Each node has at least one control point (but can have several control points).

There are three different types of nodes:

❖ **Smooth nodes** have two control points and always lie on a straight line. Whenever you move one control point, the other one moves to maintain the smoothness of the line.

❖ **Symmetrical nodes** have all of the qualities of smooth nodes, but the two control points are always equidistant from the node. As a result, the curvature on both sides of symmetrical nodes is always the same.

❖ **Cusp nodes** and their control points are not necessarily in a straight line. Therefore, you can move each control point independently, which, in effect, controls either of the segments meeting at the node. Use a cusped node when you want to make a sharp change of direction or point between two segments.

A segment can be either a line segment or a curve segment:

❖ A **line segment** uses a straight line to connect two nodes. There are no control points associated with a straight line.

❖ A **curve segment** has control points associated with it, one for each side of the node.

Now that we understand some of the terminology, let's begin shaping some curves.

1. Draw an S-shaped curve on the page using the Pencil tool.

2. To make it easier to work with, select the Zoom In tool to see the curve better.

3. Select the Shape tool from the toolbox. When your cursor becomes a black arrowhead cursor, select the node at one end of the curve.

   If it's still hard to see the node, use the Zoom In tool to zoom in on it again. You may have to click the mouse to display the nodes. Now that your curve is easy to see, let's investigate what happens when we shape the curve by dragging the node.

4. To move the node that you've selected, drag it anywhere on the screen. When you move the node, you move the position of the node relative to other nodes in the curve. However, the angles of the curve (which are governed by the control points) remain the same.

SHORTCUT

If you want to move the first node on the curve (designated by the larger node box), press the **Home** key to select it. If you want to move the last node on the curve, press the **End** key.

5. You can also shape the curve by dragging a control point. However, doing this shapes the curve in quite another manner. Dragging a control point does not change the position of the node relative to other nodes, but it does change the angle of the curve as it leaves the node.

Let's summarize how nodes and control points affect the shape of a curve:

❖ A curve always passes through its nodes.

❖ Each node has two control points, except for a node that is at the beginning or ending point of the curve.

❖ The shape of a curve between nodes is determined by the control points of each of the nodes.

❖ The control point determines the angle at which the curve meets the node.

❖ The farther a control point is from its node, the greater the curvature. Conversely, a control point closer to the node produces a shallower curve.

❖ A control point positioned directly on top of a node has no impact on the direction or shape of the curve.

❖ To create a symmetrical curve, symmetrically position the control points for the adjacent node.

The Node Edit Roll-Up Menu

The Shape tool also contains a Node Edit roll-up menu to edit individual nodes, as shown in Figure 5.31. Access this menu by double-clicking on a node or a line segment.

FIGURE 5.31 The Node Edit roll-up menu

Adding Nodes (+)

You may want to add another node to a curve. This option gives you more control over shaping the curve. You can double-click on a node or a point on a segment exactly where you want to add a node. When the Node Edit roll-up menu displays, select the **+**. A new node is displayed where you double-clicked on the node or segment. Now you can use the new node and its control points to shape your curve.

SHORTCUT

Press + on the numeric keypad to add a node.

You can also add nodes between several nodes. First, select the segments or nodes adjacent to the segments where you want to add the nodes. Either select each node while holding the **Shift** key or use the marquee-select method, which allows you to select several nodes at one time. To marquee-select several nodes, click and drag the mouse over the nodes you want to include and then release the mouse button. Then return to the Shape tool.

You can also use these two methods to select multiple objects whenever you are working with the Pick tool or the Shape tool.

Deleting Nodes (-)

You may also want to delete nodes along your curve to create a smoother shape. It is common to get unwanted extra nodes caused by extra movements you made with your mouse when you created the curve. To delete a node, double-click on the node or the line segment following the node you want to delete, and select - from the Edit Node roll-up menu. CorelDRAW deletes the node and redraws the curve.

You can press the **Del** key to delete selected nodes.

SHORTCUT

You can select and delete several nodes or segments at one time using one of the multiple select methods in conjunction with **Delete** from the menu or the **Del** key.

Joining Nodes

With the Node Edit roll-up menu, you can also join two end nodes together, closing an open path.

1. Select the nodes you want to join, either by using the marquee-select method or by holding the **Shift** key while you select each of them.

2. Double-click on one of the selected nodes.

3. Select the Chainlinks icon from the Node Edit roll-up menu. The two end nodes are joined, and the curve is recreated as a closed path.

You can also join the end nodes from two separate paths to create one continuous path. First, however, you must make them part of the same object.

1. Select both objects either by using the marquee-select method or by holding the **Shift** key while you select each object.

2. Choose **Combine** from the Arrange menu. The two objects will be joined. Although the objects look the same, they function as one object. The status line now reads *Curve* instead of *2 objects selected*.

3. Switch to the Shape tool and use the marquee-select method to select the two end nodes that you want to join.

4. Double-click on one of the selected nodes and choose the Chain-links icon Join from the Node Edit roll-up menu. The curve is drawn as a single path.

Breaking Curves

You can also use the Node Edit roll-up menu to break a curve at a single node.

1. Double-click at the node or the spot along a segment where you want to break the curve.

2. Select the Broken Chain icon on the Node Edit roll-up menu. The curve is broken at that point, and two nodes appear, superimposed upon each other.

Once you've broken a closed path it becomes an open path and you cannot fill it.

N O T E

You can also break a curve at several points simultaneously by selecting all the nodes where you want to break the curve. Double-click on one of the nodes and select the Broken Chain icon. The curve separates at all those nodes.

Auto-Reduce

The **Auto-Reduce** option automatically deletes extraneous nodes.

To Line

The **To Line** option converts a curve to a straight line. Follow these steps to convert a curve to a straight line:

1. Double-click on the curve segment or its end node with the Shape tool.

2. Select **To Line** from the Edit Node roll-up menu. The control points disappear, and the line segment changes to a straight line.

To Curve

The **To Curve** option converts a straight line to a curve. Follow these steps to convert a line to a curve:

1. Double-click on the line segment or its node with the Shape tool.

2. Select **To Curve** from the Edit Node roll-up menu.

3. Two segments appear on the line, indicating that it is a curve (although it still appears straight). You may now reshape the curve.

As with many of the other options on the Node Edit roll-up menu, you can apply **To Curve** or **To Line** to multiple segments.

Stretching and Scaling

You can stretch and scale selected parts of a curve, just as you can stretch and scale objects. To stretch and scale a curve:

1. Select two or more nodes.
2. Click on the **Stretch** option. Eight sizing handles are displayed.
3. Stretch or scale the node just as you would an object.

Rotating and Skewing

You can rotate and skew parts of a curve, just as you can rotate and skew objects. To rotate or skew nodes:

1. Select the node you want to rotate.
2. Click on **Rotate**. Eight rotating and skewing handles are displayed.
3. Use the rotating and skewing handles just as you would for an object.

Changing Node Types

The Node Edit roll-up menu also has options that change the type of node to **Cusp**, **Smooth**, or **Symmetrical**. To change the node type:

1. Double-click on the node you want to change.
2. Select the new type of node from the roll-up menu.

Remember that symmetrical, smooth, and cusped nodes are characterized by the control points of the node.

Align

The Node Edit roll-up menu has an **Align** option that lets you vertically or horizontally align multiple nodes to make it easier for multiple shapes to share the same outline. To align multiple nodes:

1. Select both nodes.

2. Click on one and select **Align** from the roll-up menu.

3. When prompted, select **Align Horizontal**, **Align Vertical**, or **Align Control Points** and then click on **OK**. The nodes are aligned in the manner you specified.

If the two nodes you want to align are in separate objects, you'll first need to combine them before you can align them.

Elastic Mode

The **Elastic Mode** option changes the way multiple selected nodes move when dragged with the mouse. If you select this option, the curve appears to behave like a rubber band, expanding and contracting with the movement of the mouse.

Arranging Objects

When you create a drawing with CorelDRAW, your graphic is not just a result of the objects you choose and their coordinate positions, but their positions relative to each other. You can place objects in front of or behind other objects, align several objects in a variety of positions, group or ungroup two or more objects, or combine several objects into one curve and later break them apart.

Aligning Objects

You may want to *align* your objects, that is, line them up in a certain direction. Even though you could do that by carefully placing them with your mouse according to your rulers and your grid, CorelDRAW provides a much easier method. Draw the objects shown in Figure 5.32, and let's see how we can align the different elements.

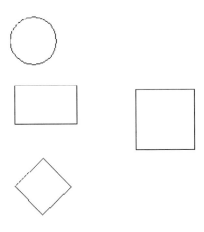

FIGURE 5.32 Drawing of shapes

The objects don't quite line up, but we can fix that.

1. Use the Pick tool to select the objects you want to align.

2. Choose the circle at the top and the rectangle directly under it.

3. Select **Align** from the Arrange menu. The Align dialog box, shown in Figure 5.33, is displayed.

SHORTCUT

Press **Ctrl-A** to open the Align dialog box.

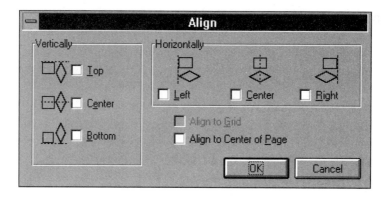

FIGURE 5.33 *The Align dialog box*

4. Look at the objects shown with handles in Figure 5.34. If you want the circle centered over the rectangle, select **Center** from the Horizontally section on the right side of the Align dialog box. Click on **OK**, and the two objects line up correctly, as displayed in Figure 5.34.

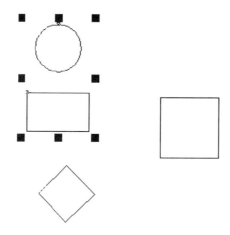

FIGURE 5.34 *Aligned circle and rectangle*

5. First, select the objects, then align the diamond and the square vertically, select **Center** from the Vertically section of the Align dialog box and click on **OK**. The two objects line up, as shown in Figure 5.35.

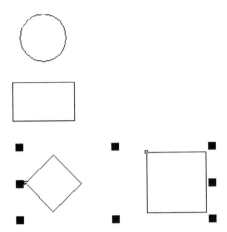

FIGURE 5.35 *An aligned diamond and rectangle*

6. You can also align objects in two directions at a time. Choose the diamond and the circle. From the Align dialog box, select **Right** and **Bottom**. Click on **OK**, and the objects are aligned on the bottom right.

If you select your objects using the mouse and the **Shift** key, the last object that you select is the basis of the alignment. All other selected objects are aligned with it. However, if you select your object with the marquee-select method, the first object that you created is the basis of the alignment. Unless you have a very good memory and know which object you created first, you may want to select your objects with the **Shift** key to make your results more predictable.

If you select **Align to Grid** or **Align to Center of Page**, the aligned objects are repositioned as a group to the grid or the center of the page, respectively.

N O T E

Changing an Object's Position

If you've included many objects in your drawing, you'll find that the graphic looks quite different, depending upon which object is in the foreground and which object is in the background. To get an idea about how different a graphic can look, let's look at a couple of views of the same objects in Figures 5.36 and 5.37.

FIGURE 5.36 *The sea horse in the background*

FIGURE 5.37 *The sea horse in the foreground*

The Arrange menu has several options to help you order your objects. You can place objects in front of or behind others, or you can bring an object to the foreground or background of a graphic. To illustrate many of the options in the Arrange menu, we'll use the row of horses shown in Figure 5.38.

FIGURE 5.38 *A row of horses*

If you want to bring a particular object to the foreground, select it using the Pick tool, open the Arrange menu, and select **To Front** from the Order fly-out menu. In the example shown here, selecting the dark horse before choosing **To Front** places it on top of all the other horses, as shown in Figure 5.39.

FIGURE 5.39 A row of horses with the dark horse in front

Press **Shift-PgUp** to select the **To Front** option.

You can also use the Arrange menu to place an object in the background. Select the object using the Pick tool and then choose the **To Back** option.

Press **Shift-PgDn** to select **To Back**.

The **Forward One** and **Back One** options are similar to the **To Front** and **To Back** options. However, instead of bringing the selected object on top of (or behind) all the other objects, it simply advances or retreats the object one position.

Press **Ctrl-PgUp** to select **Forward One**. Press **Ctrl-PgDn** to select **Back One**.

Finally, you can reverse the order of several selected objects. Select all the horses and then select **Reverse Order** from the Arrange menu. You can see the result in Figure 5.40.

FIGURE 5.40 A row of horses in reverse order

Grouping Objects

You can group several objects so that you can treat them as a single object. This is similar to using the marquee-select method or selecting multiple objects using the **Shift** key. In fact, you'll need to select the objects that make up your group before you can actually apply the **Group** option from the Arrange menu.

Once the objects are grouped, you can move, resize, rotate, or skew the group without changing any of the objects' relative positions. You can tell by the status line whether you have multiple objects selected. If you have a group of objects selected, the status line reads *Group of 6 objects on layer 1*.

Press **Ctrl-G** to group objects, then click the mouse.

SHORTCUT

You can also group two or more groups or groups and individual objects using the same technique.

N O T E

One disadvantage to a group is that you can't separately edit the individual objects. Therefore, you may at some time want to ungroup them. Select the group and then select **Ungroup** from the Arrange menu. The status line reflects the number of objects selected.

If you have other groups embedded within the group, you may need to ungroup them as well.

N O T E

Press **Ctrl-U** to ungroup the group, then click the mouse.

SHORTCUT

Combining Objects

The **Combine** and **Break Apart** options are similar to the **Group** and **Ungroup** options. There is one important difference. Combine converts all the selected objects to a single curved object, and the status line reflects the fact that one curve is currently selected.

Select all the objects you want to combine and then select **Combine** from the Arrange menu.

There are several advantages to combining objects:

❖ You can edit all the objects as one object.

❖ You can use the Shape tool to edit several nodes at once in the newly created curve, even though the line segments are not attached.

❖ You can conserve memory by combining complex objects.

❖ Combining objects can create interesting effects such as masking, with multiple overlaid objects.

To take the object apart, select the object and choose **Break Apart**. The curve then appears as a series of separate objects, and the number of objects selected is reflected in the status line.

SHORTCUT

Press **Ctrl-K** to take the objects apart.

Separating Objects and Converting Objects to Curves

The **Weld** option joins objects where they intersect. This command removes sections of paths that were once between those points.

The **Intersection** option joins the paths of objects where they intersect.

The **Trim** option separates object paths at intersections. You may have to move a trimmed object to see the effect.

The **Separate** option breaks apart objects that you created with a blend (discussed in *Chapter 8*) or separates text that has been fitted to a path.

The **Convert to Curves** option converts text, ellipses, and rectangles to curved objects that you can manipulate with the Shape tool. You can convert text to a graphic using **Convert To Curves**, which allows full editing capability of all Bézier curve nodes and control points.

Layers

You can superimpose objects on top of each other by placing them on different layers. Generally, only one layer is active at a time, which means that you can work on only one layer at a time with your commands. However, all of the layers are part of your drawing, and you can switch among layers. You can also make layers invisible (and then make them visible again) or print individual layers rather than the entire graphic.

To manage the different layers in your drawing, use the Layers roll-up menu, found on the Layout menu.

FIGURE 5.41 The Layers roll-up menu

Layer 1 is the default layer, which means that unless you create another layer, all your work appears on Layer 1.

The grid and guidelines are on their own separate layers, but they govern your work in all of the layers that you create.

NOTE

To create a new layer, click on the black right arrowhead in the Layers roll-up menu and select **New** from the fly-out menu. The New Layer dialog box, shown in Figure 5.42, is displayed, allowing you to set the options Layer 2.

FIGURE 5.42 The New Layer dialog box

By default, the layer that you are creating is visible. To make it invisible, click on the **Visible** check box in the Options section of the New Layers dialog box. When you are drawing a complex graphic, you may want to put part of it on an invisible layer.

The **Printable** option is also selected by default, but you can deselect a layer so that the layer and the objects on it are excluded when printing the graphic.

You can also select the **Locked** option to prevent you from altering the objects on a layer. You may find this useful if you spent a lot of time and effort creating an object or group of objects and do not want to alter them by mistake while you're working on other parts of your graphic. Place the object on its own locked layer and proceed with your work.

The **Color Override** option lets you assign a color to all objects in the layer but creates the color as a wireframe outline. This option may be helpful, especially while you are creating your drawings, because it identifies the objects by layer, yet leaves them transparent, so that you can see all of the objects underneath. If you are working with a great many layers, it's a good idea to assign a separate color to each layer, so that you can easily choose the objects you want.

Each new layer is automatically numbered consecutively, and the name of each layer is its assigned number. However, you can rename the layer using up to 32 characters.

Now that you've created Layer 2, let's place an object on it so that we can see how layers behave.

1. Make sure that Layer 2 is active by selecting it in the Layers roll-up menu.

2. Create an ellipse and fill it with gray, so that we know where it is. The ellipse on Layer 2 is shown in Figure 5.43. The status line indicates that the currently selected object is an ellipse on Layer 2.

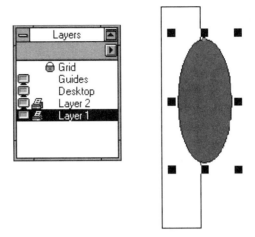

FIGURE 5.43 Layer 2 with a gray ellipse

3. Since the top-named layer is always the top in the stack of layers, we can expect that the Layer 1 objects is superimposed on top of the shaded ellipse. Press **F9** to preview your graphic and verify that the layers are ordered correctly.

You can also perform other editing functions with the Layers roll-up menu. When you click on the black right arrow, you can delete the active layer (the layer selected in the Layer roll-up menu) by choosing **Delete** from the fly-out menu.

When you delete a layer, the next layer in the stack becomes the active layer.

N O T E

You can also use this menu to move or copy an object from one layer to another. Select the object that you want to move or copy. Then, make sure that you select the destination layer in the Layers roll-up menu and click on **Move To** or **Copy To** from the fly-out menu. The object is transferred to the new layer.

N O T E

Copy To leaves the object on the original layer, while **Move To** removes it from the original layer.

If you want to be able to work on all the layers at the same time, click on the **Multi-Layer** option. You then select any object, regardless of which layer it's on.

You can also change the stacking order of the layers. For example, to make Layer 2 the top layer, click on Layer 2 in the roll-up menu and, while pressing the mouse button, move Layer 2 up over Layer 1. Notice that Layer 2 is now at the top of the list. If you press **F9** to preview your drawing, you'll see that the objects on Layer 2 are superimposed on the Layer 1 objects.

Summary

In this chapter you learned about lines and curves, some of the basic building blocks in CorelDRAW. You also saw how to use the Pick tool to modify, move, and manipulate objects. You saw how easy it is to manipulate objects and to apply outline and fill to any CorelDRAW object. You can use the objects that you created to compose many different graphics. You also learned how to use layers to dynamically arrange objects.

Chapter 6

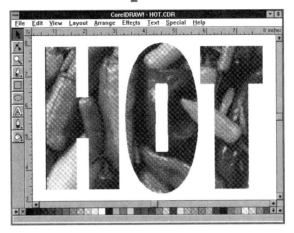

The Write Type: Using Text

Text can take the form of artistic lettering or paragraph text, and you can either create it in CorelDRAW or import it from a word processing application. CorelDRAW also has many powerful editing features such as bullet lists, text flow between frames, spelling and thesaurus utilities, and a typing assistant.

This chapter covers:

❖ Artistic text

❖ Editing text

❖ Modifying tex

❖ Paragraph text

❖ The Text roll-up menu

❖ Fitting text to a path

❖ Kerning

❖ Spell Check, Thesaurus, Find, Replace, and Type Assist

❖ Merging print

❖ Symbols

113

Artistic Text

If you plan to create special effects with your text, you'll need to use artistic text. Artistic text is best suited for incorporating small amounts of text into your graphics. Each block of artistic text is limited to 250 characters. When you need to add more text, either begin another block of text or use paragraph text.

Let's begin with placing text in your graphic:

1. From the toolbox, select the Text tool, represented by an *A*. Click and hold the mouse button. Figure 6.1 shows the Text tool fly-out menu.

FIGURE 6.1 The Text tool fly-out menu

2. Click on the page to position the cursor.
3. Type in your text.

Press **F8** to select the Text tool.

SHORTCUT

While you are typing, you can use any of the normal Windows editing keys to modify your text, including **Backspace** to erase what you've done.

You can also change the contents of the text string directly on the screen by clicking on the text while the Text tool is selected. To erase a portion of the text, highlight it and then press **Del**.

Editing Text

Once you've entered text, you can change any of its attributes (such as its style or font) by selecting the text with the Pick tool and then selecting **Edit Text** from the Text menu. The Edit Text dialog box is displayed, as shown in Figure 6.2.

SHORTCUT

Press **Ctrl-Shift-T** to access the Edit Text dialog box.

FIGURE 6.2 The Edit Text dialog box

The top part of the dialog box contains a text entry box that allows you to enter or edit text. The scroll arrows allow you to move up and down in this entry box. While you are in the text entry window, you can use any of the following keys:

- ❖ **Backspace** deletes the character to the left of the cursor.
- ❖ **Del** deletes the character to the right of the cursor or any text that you highlight with your mouse.
- ❖ **Left and Right Arrows** move your cursor through the text.
- ❖ **Home** brings your cursor to the beginning of the current line.

❖ **End** brings your cursor to the end of the current line.

❖ **PgUp** brings your cursor to the first line of the text string or paragraph.

❖ **PgDn** brings your cursor to the last line in the text entry window.

❖ **Enter** begins a new line.

Click on Character below the text entry box to open the Character Attributes dialog box, which is shown in Figure 6.3. This dialog box has a preview window, showing how the text looks in the font you have selected. To the left is a list of the fonts available. There are 49 typefaces included with CorelDRAW. You can also include others that are in compatible formats or create your own. If you have a CD ROM, you have access to 750 fonts in both TIF and PFB formats. With most standard typefaces, you can choose normal, italic, bold, or bold-italic styling by clicking on the style names from the style drop-down list.

Not all typefaces have all styles available.

N O T E

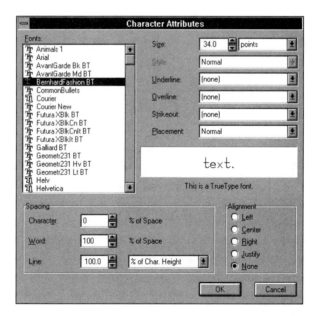

FIGURE 6.3 The Character Attributes dialog box

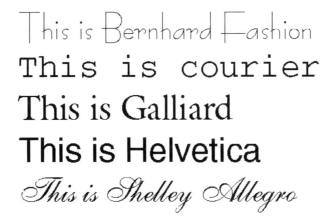

FIGURE 6.4 Examples of typefaces

Notice that you can scroll through the list of fonts (and watch the preview box change) to help you make a selection (see Figure 6.4).

Select a point size in the size box, either by using the scroll bar or by entering a value.

You can choose to align your text to the left, right, or center, to both margins (justified), or not at all by clicking on the appropriate Alignment radio buttons. Examples of text alignment are shown in Figure 6.5.

This
is
left
justification

This
is
center
justification

This
is
right
justification

FIGURE 6.5 Examples of text alignment.

Adjust the spacing by entering values in the **Character**, **Word**, and **Line** spacing fields. All of the values you enter in these fields are a percentage of the point size.

Character spacing determines the space between each character. The default value is **0**. If you make the value positive, the spacing between characters increases. If you make the value negative, the spacing decreases. Figure 6.6 shows examples of character spacing.

This is 0 percent character spacing

This is 50 percent character spacing

This is 100 percent character spacing

FIGURE 6.6 Examples of character spacing

Word spacing works in much the same way, except that the default values start at **100**, which means that the space between each word is the size of a character. Figure 6.7 shows examples of word spacing.

This is 0 percentwordspacing

This is 100 percent word spacing

This is 200 percent word spacing

FIGURE 6.7 Examples of word spacing

Line spacing is the space between the baseline of one line to the baseline of the next line. Proper line spacing keeps the bottoms of the lowest character from touching the top of the highest character on the next line.

Modifying Text

You've already used the Pick tool to move, stretch, shrink, rotate, skew, and mirror objects such as rectangles, ellipses, lines, and curves. The Pick tool performs the same operations on your text. Type in the sample text shown in Figure 6.8.

Sample text

FIGURE 6.8 Sample text

With the text selected, click on the Pick tool. Drag the text by one of the corner handles to scale the text object proportionally. If you check the status line, you'll notice the point size has changed. You can also stretch or shrink text by dragging on one of the middle handles. The point size changes although the text is not stretched proportionally, as shown in Figure 6.9.

Sample text

FIGURE 6.9 Stretched text

Double-click on the nodes of the object to display the double-headed arrows that allow you to rotate and skew the text. Drag one of the corner handles to rotate the object, as shown in Figure 6.10. Now try dragging one of the middle handles to skew the object, as shown in Figure 6.11. You can also create a mirror image of the text by dragging a square middle handle either vertically or horizontally through the selected text string, as shown in Figure 6.12.

FIGURE 6.10 A rotated text object

FIGURE 6.11 A skewed text object

txet ɘlqmɒꙄ

FIGURE 6.12 A mirrored text object

Any CorelDRAW action that you can perform on objects such as ellipses, rectangles, lines, and curves can also be performed on text. You can also stretch, shrink, scale, rotate, skew, and mirror objects by entering numerical values in any of the dialog boxes under the Effects menu.

Paragraph Text

If you're planning to enter a large block of data, use paragraph text. As many as 4000 characters fit in a paragraph of text. A *paragraph* is any block of text that ends in a carriage return.

To enter paragraph text:

1. Select the Paragraph icon from the Text tool fly-out menu.
2. Click on your page, and a text frame is created, as shown in Figure 6.13. You can also create a text frame by clicking on the top left margin and dragging to the lower right margin.

FIGURE 6.13 A paragraph text frame

3. Type text directly into the frame. Text automatically wraps within the frame, as it does in a word processor.

Paragraph text can be edited and formatted the same way artistic text is formatted.

Wrapping Paragraph Text Around an Object

See the section on envelopes in *Chapter 8* to wrap paragraph text around an object.

Flowing Text Between Frames

Text can flow between frames on the same page or between pages in multiple-page documents. Frames are dynamically linked so that if the dimensions of one link frame are changed, the text flow automatically adjusts in the remaining frames. Imported text can also be flowed.

To flow text between frames:

1. Create your first frame and select it with the Pick tool. (You do not need to have text in it, but you may if you like.) Hollow boxes are displayed on both the top and the bottom of the selected frame, as shown in Figure 6.14.

FIGURE 6.14 A selected paragraph text frame with hollow boxes displayed

2. Click on the top hollow box to flow text from the beginning of the frame or click on the bottom hollow box to flow text from the end of the frame. A text flow icon is displayed.

3. If text is to flow on the same page, click and drag the icon from the desired upper-left margin of the new text box to the lower-left margin and release. Text will now be dynamically linked from one box to the other.

4. To flow text between frames on separate pages, use the page selector in the bottom scroll bar to select the destination page. Then, create the linked text box as described in Step 3.

Another way to select paragraph text is to use the Pick tool. Then, choose the **Edit Text** option from the Edit menu (or press **Ctrl-Shift-T**) and click on the Paragraph button to access the Paragraph dialog box.

The Paragraph dialog box has four tabs: Spacing, Tabs, Indents, and Bullet.

❖ **Spacing**. Controls the spacing for individual paragraphs in a text frame. The Spacing options work as described earlier. They may also be used to adjust the spacing of artistic text. The **Before Paragraph** and **After Paragraph** options control the spacing above and below the selected paragraph(s). Spacing options are shown in Figure 6.15.

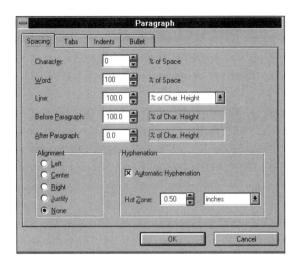

FIGURE 6.15 *The Paragraph dialog box with the Spacing tab selected*

❖ **Tabs**. Tab stops are preset at 0.5-inch intervals. Change these settings by selecting tab **Alignment** and then clicking the tabs into position on the ruler. Tab settings may also be applied numerically by typing the value into the box to the right of the Apply Tabs Every button and then clicking on Set. Tab options are shown in Figure 6.16.

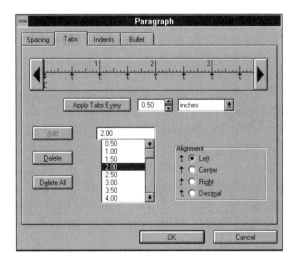

FIGURE 6.16 *The Paragraph dialog box with the Tabs tab selected*

❖ **Indents**. **First Line** indicates a value for indenting the first line. Indents for subsequent lines may be specified with the **Rest Of Lines** option. You can use the ruler, as with tab settings, or the numeric pad. Indent options are shown in Figure 6.17.

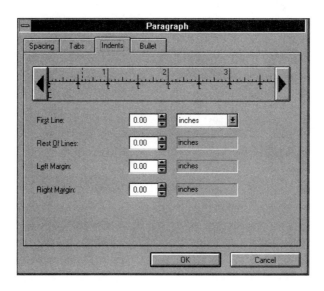

FIGURE 6.17 The Paragraph dialog box with the Indents tab selected

❖ **Bullet**. Paragraphs may be defined as bullet lists so the bullet aligns with the left margin. Items in a bullet list should be indicated by pressing the **Enter** key after each one. Select **Bullet On**, click on the symbol category you want to use, and then choose the settings you want. Any symbol may be used as a bullet. The bullet symbol is displayed with the same format as your text. Bullet options are shown in Figure 6.18.

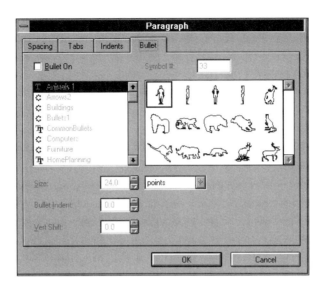

FIGURE 6.18 The Paragraph dialog box with the Bullet tab selected

In addition to typing in text using the Artistic Text and Paragraph Text tools, there are two other methods of bringing text into CorelDRAW. You can either paste text, which you can use for both artistic and paragraph text, or you can import text, which works with paragraph text only.

Pasting Text

Before you can paste text, you must cut or copy it into the Windows clipboard either from another text box in CorelDRAW or from any other Windows package that is compatible with the clipboard. Cut (**Shift-Del**) removes text and puts it on the clipboard. Copy (**Ctrl-Insert**) copies the text to the clipboard.

To paste text into CorelDRAW, select **Paste** from the Edit menu or press **Shift-Insert**. Any text in the clipboard is pasted into the dialog box.

If there are more than 250 characters in the clipboard, the text is automatically placed as paragraph text.

You must already have text entered in your text string in your frame, regardless of whether you are working with artistic or paragraph text. If necessary, enter just one character. As soon as you import the clipboard text, you can delete this extraneous starting character. Any characters over the 4000 character limit are deleted.

The pasted text has all of the currently selected attributes, such as font, size, alignment, and spacing.

Importing Text

Another way to bring text into CorelDRAW is to import it. You can use only the **Import** option for paragraph text. You must already have created a paragraph frame and have at least one character entered in it. From the File menu, select **Import**, and the Import dialog box is displayed.

Under **File Name**, you'll see that the file name extension *.TXT is specified. Scroll through the List Files of Type box to see other types of files that you can import. You can import only those files that are saved in ASCII or generic format. Most word processors have the capability of saving files this way. To import files correctly, avoid including tabs and indents in the original file.

If you do not see the file you want in the drive and directory listed, change the drive by scrolling through the drive box and clicking on the directory that contains your file. Select the file you wish to import and click on **OK**. The text is displayed in the text entry box.

Once you have imported your text, you can edit it either on the screen or in the text entry box. However, text over the 8000-character limit is deleted.

The Text Roll-Up Menu

Once you have text on the screen, you can manipulate it using options from the Text menu.

The first item in the Text menu is the Text roll-up menu, which is shown in Figure 6.19. You can use the Text roll-up menu to format both artistic and paragraph text.

FIGURE 6.19 The Text roll-up menu

Press **Ctrl-F2** to display the Text roll-up menu.

To make room on your screen, roll up the menu by using the up arrow in the upper-right corner of the menu. To restore the menu, click on the down arrow. You can also move the menu around the screen to make viewing the document easier.

Options in the Text roll-up menu include:

❖ **Font**. The first box shows the currently selected font. To select a different font, click on the drop-down arrow and select one from the list shown.

❖ **Style**. You select text style using the style drop-down arrow. Select bold, italic, subscript, or superscript. Not all styles are available with all fonts.

❖ **Size**. You can increase or decrease the point size by clicking on the up or down scroll arrow or by changing the point size value.

❖ **Alignment**. You can change the text alignment using one of the five buttons in the middle of the roll-up menu.

❖ **Frame**. You can use the **Frame** option to divide a text frame into columns. Click on **Frame** to specify the number of columns you want and to specify the *gutter width* (the space between columns). This option is also available by selecting **Frame** from the Text menu.

❖ **Paragraph**. You can select the **Paragraph** option to format paragraph text. Position the insertion point anywhere in the paragraph(s) you wish to format and then click on **Paragraph** to access the Paragraph dialog box. The Paragraph dialog box can also be accessed from the Text menu.

❖ **Character Attributes**. Click on **Character Attributes** to open the Character dialog box. You may use this dialog box to apply character formatting to your text.

Changing Character Attributes

You can change the attributes of any character or characters you selected with the Shape tool or highlighted with your cursor.

Look at the text shown in Figure 6.20. If, for example, you want to enlarge only the letter *X* and make it bold, select the Shape tool and then click on the letter *X*.

FIGURE 6.20 Changing attributes of only part of the text

Double-click on the *X* character. The Character Attributes dialog box is displayed, as shown in Figure 6.21. Now set the font, font style, placement, angle, and shift of the selected character(s). You can also access the Character

Attributes dialog box through the **Character** option on the Text menu. An abbreviated version of this dialog box is available by selecting **Character Attributes** from the Text roll-up menu.

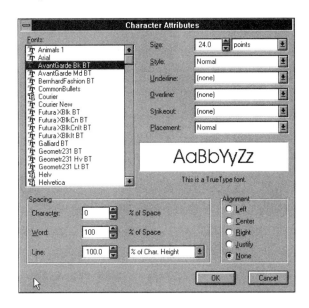

FIGURE 6.21 The Character Attributes dialog box

Fitting Text to a Path

Interesting and attractive effects are created when you fit text to a path. You can format text around ellipses, rectangles, or curves, as shown in the example in Figure 6.22.

FIGURE 6.22 Text fitted to an ellipse

To fit text to a path:

1. Create both the text and the path to which you want the text fitted, as shown in Figure 6.23.

The text must be created using the Artistic Text tool. Paragraph text cannot be fit to a path.

N O T E

FIGURE 6.23 Text and a curve

2. Select the path and the text; then, select **Fit Text To Path** from the Text menu to open the Fit Text To Path roll-up menu, which is shown in Figure 6.24.

FIGURE 6.24 The Fit Text To Path roll-up menu

SHORTCUT

Press **Ctrl-F** to open the Fit Text To Path roll-up menu.

3. Select the variables you need and click on **Apply**.
4. The text is fitted around the path, as shown in Figure 6.25.

FIGURE 6.25 Text fitted to a path

The best way to work with the Fit Text To Path roll-up menu is to make your selections from all three drop-down menus before you apply them. Then, take a look at how the text appears fitted on the path. If you don't like its appearance, you can go back and revise the selections.

You can also change the shape of the path. If you want to change the path, select the path and its attached text; then, select **Separate** from the Arrange menu and modify the path. After you modify the path, you can refit the text to the new path. If you modify the text, the new text is fitted to the path.

After you place your text on the path, you might want to remove the path. Select the text, choose **Separate** from the Arrange menu, select the path, and then delete it. The text is still fitted to the now invisible path. You can also leave your path in place by changing both its fill and outline to **None**, so that the path is not displayed or printed.

To fit your text to another character, as shown in Figure 6.26, you must first make the target letter a curve by selecting **Convert To Curves (Ctrl-Q)** from the Arrange menu.

FIGURE 6.26 *Text fitted to a character*

Let's look at the options in the Text roll-up menu and see how they affect the results when you fit your text to a path.

Characters Rotated to Path Baseline

The first drop-down menu in the Fit Text To Path roll-up menu, which is shown in Figure 6.27, selects how the text sits on a path. The options are visually represented, so you can easily choose which one fits your needs.

FIGURE 6.27 *Options for text to sit on a path*

❖ Rotating letters makes the letters in the text follow the contours of the path. CorelDRAW may skew some of the letters in the text both horizontally and vertically to match the curvature of the path.

❖ To skew the letters vertically to fit the path, choose the second option in the drop-down menu. The degree of skew is proportional to the slope of the path.

❖ To skew the letters horizontally, choose the third option in the drop-down menu. Again, the slope of the path determines the degree of skew.

❖ The fourth option maintains the letters in their upright position, regardless of the curvature of the path.

Text and Path Distance

The second drop-down menu in the Fit Text To Path roll-up menu specifies the distance of the text from the path. Again, the drop-down menu, which is shown in Figure 6.28, shows all of the options.

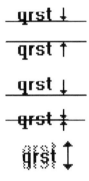

FIGURE 6.28 *Options for the distance of the text from the path*

❖ The first option places the text directly on the path baseline.

❖ You can also place the string below the path, but not touching the path.

❖ To place the text above the path without touching the path, select the third option. CorelDRAW calculates how far from the path the text sits.

❖ The fourth option places the text on the centerline of the path.

❖ You have the option of determining how far the text appears above or below the path. Click on the fifth option to move the text the desired distance from the path.

You can also specify an exact distance, in inches, that the text sits above or below the path. Click on **Edit** in the Fit Text To Path roll-up menu. In the **Distance From Path** field enter a positive value for distance above the path or a negative value for distance below the path.

Text Path Alignment

The third drop-down menu in the Fit Text To Path roll-up menu is shown in Figure 6.29. Here you can adjust the text's alignment to the path. Alignment behaves differently depending on the type of path you are using. For paths that are not true ellipses or rectangles, but including all other closed paths, there are three possibilities:

❖ By default, the text is placed at the starting node of the path.

❖ You can also center your text on the path, which positions the text midway between the starting and ending nodes of the path.

❖ The third alignment option fits the text to the last node of the path.

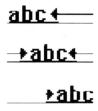

FIGURE 6.29 *Options for alignment of text on a path*

For true ellipse and rectangle objects (those drawn with the Ellipse and Rectangle tools), the Path Alignment drop-down menu is replaced with a square icon containing a circle, which is divided into four sections. Click on the section in which you want the text to appear, and the text appears in that portion of the rectangle or ellipse.

You can also specify the distance that the text is offset from the starting point of the curve. Click on **Edit** in the Fit Text To Path roll-up menu. In the **Horizontal Offset** field, enter a positive value for the distance to the right of the starting point or a negative value for the distance to the left of the starting point.

Place on Other Side

The last option in the Fit Text To Path roll-up menu is **Place On Other Side**. This check box reverses all of the specifications you made. Your text is aligned on the opposite side of the path with the text mirrored, as shown in Figure 6.30.

FIGURE 6.30 Text fitted to a path and placed on other side

Other Text Adjustments

After you have fitted text to a path, you can adjust it by altering either the path or the text. Once you have fitted text to a path, it is interactively linked. Any adjustment you make to the text or path causes the text to be refitted to the path.

To move or kern characters without modifying the path, drag the text along the path by using the Shape tool, highlighting all of the nodes in the text and dragging them to the desired location. You can also adjust the individual character spacing or *kerning* for the text along the path. Use the Shape tool to move the individual (or a group) of characters along the path.

You may also need to adjust the angles of some of the characters to compensate for their new positions along the path.

This method is fine if you need to change only one or two characters. If you need to adjust several characters to achieve a better fit, it may be easier to first return the text to a straight baseline, make your adjustments, and then refit the text to the path. Undo the **Fit Text To Path** command, make adjustments to the text, and then select **Fit Text To Path** again.

There can be no intervening command between **Fit Text To Path** and **Undo**.

N O T E

This will often be a repetitive, trial-and-error sequence until you are satisfied with the arrangement. Once you are approaching perfection and need to adjust the spacing on only a few characters, use the Shape tool to kern your characters.

To start over, you can also use the **Straighten Text** option in the Text menu to return your text to a straight baseline. Select the text by holding the **Ctrl** key while you click on the text and then select **Straighten Text** from the Text menu. This procedure readjusts characters you rotated or shifted after you fitted the text to the path. All of your original spacing will be lost.

Another way of retracing your steps is to realign the text to the baseline. Select the text by holding the **Ctrl** key while you click on the text. Then, select **Align To Baseline Text** from the Text menu. This option resets any vertical shift you applied to your characters, but it does not affect any horizontal shift. It can give you some interesting results.

Any rotation done to your characters will be lost.

NOTE

Kerning

To interactively work with an individual character within the text, select the string with the Shape tool. Notice the nodes next to each letter. In addition to these nodes, spacing control handles are displayed at each end of the last line of artistic text.

To help you interactively kern text, you may wish to zoom in on the string you're working with. Your spacing will be much more accurate if you work with a close-up of your text, as shown in Figure 6.31.

FIGURE 6.31 *Zoomed-in text with nodes*

N O T E

If you have selected paragraph text, the spacing control handles appear at the bottom of the text frame.

You can move a character by selecting its node and dragging it to a new position. You can also use the arrow keys on your keyboard to move the character. If you hold down an arrow key, the character repeats, that is, it moves in continuous small steps for as long as you hold down the key.

You can also work with several characters at once by either using the marquee-select method or pressing the **Shift** key while you click.

If you are working with paragraph text, use the marquee-select method or the shift-and-click method to select characters and then move the text to a new location.

Spell Checker, Thesaurus, Find, Replace, and Type Assist

You want the text in your graphics to have artistic attributes as well as to be accurate. There are two options on the Text menu, **Spell Checker** and **Thesaurus**, to help you.

Spell Checker

You can check the spelling of either a single word or a block of text. Select **Spell Checker** from the Text menu, and the dialog box shown in Figure 6.32 is displayed.

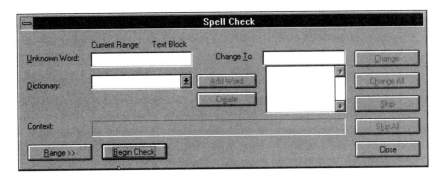

FIGURE 6.32 Spell Checker dialog box

You can select text in the following ways:

❖ To check only a few words in the text, select the Text tool and then use the mouse to highlight the words you need to check. Click on the Highlighted Text button in the Spell Checker Range area of the dialog box. (If the Range area is not displayed, click on the **Range >>** button.)

❖ To check all the artistic or paragraph text, you can select the text with the Pick tool and click on the Text Block button in the Spell Checker Range area of the dialog box.

❖ You may also use the **All Document Text** option in the Spell Check Range area to check all text in a document.

Click on **Begin Check**, and CorelDRAW begins checking the selected words. If the words are found in the dictionary, the message *Spelling check finished. No spelling errors found.* is displayed. Click on **Close** to return to your normal screen.

If the word is not in the dictionary, the word appears in the **Unknown Word** field. If there are several unrecognizable words in the text you're checking, the spelling checker presents the next unrecognized word as soon as you take action on the current word.

When a word is not found, you have several options:

❖ **Skip**. You do not want to replace the word. The next unrecognized word is displayed.

❖ **Skip All**. The spelling checker ignores this word and all later occurrences of the word. The next unrecognized word is displayed.

❖ **Change**. If the spelling checker cannot suggest an alternative or does not present the right alternative for you, you can enter the correction in the **Change To** box and click on **Change** to replace the word in your text.

❖ **Change All**. If you want to replace all occurrences of the misspelled word in your text, click on **Change All**.

The spelling checker does not check your replacement word.

Although the spelling checker's dictionary is quite large (it is a Houghton-Mifflin dictionary containing approximately 116,000 words), you may need to create your own supplemental dictionary. This may be especially helpful if you are working in a specialized field, or if you use many acronyms, abbreviations, or foreign words. To create a personal dictionary, click on **Create**, and Create

Personal Dictionary dialog box comes up. Enter file name. Click on **Add Word** to add the word to your personal dictionary. You may have multiple personal dictionaries for different purposes.

When the spelling checker is finished, it displays a message indicating that it has checked all of the words. Click **OK**, and you are returned to your CorelDRAW screen.

If you wish to exit the spelling checker before it is finished checking all the text, click on **Close**. All replacements made by the spelling checker remain in effect.

Thesaurus

You can use the thesaurus to suggest alternate words, or *synonyms*, for over-used words.

With the Text tool selected, highlight a word in a text string and then click on **Thesaurus** in the Text menu. The Thesaurus dialog box is displayed, as shown in Figure 6.33.

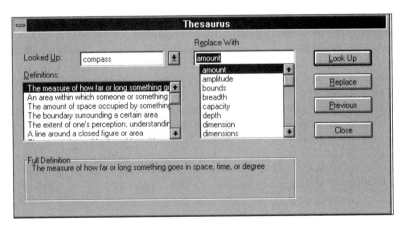

FIGURE 6.33 Thesaurus dialog box

The word that you highlighted is displayed in the Looked Up field.

You can also use the thesaurus with no word highlighted. Enter the word that you want to look up in the **Looked Up** field and click on **Look Up**.

If the word is found in the thesaurus, its definitions and synonyms are displayed in the two boxes. Click on the alternate that you need and then click on **Replace**. The word is replaced in the text with its synonym.

To close the thesaurus, click on **Close**. This does not reverse any replacements you have made.

Finding Text

To find text:

1. Insert your cursor in a text block.

2. Select **Find** from the Text menu. The Find dialog box is displayed, as shown in Figure 6.34.

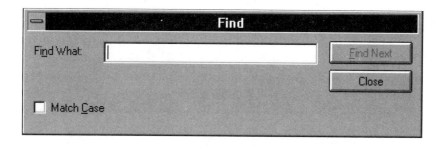

FIGURE 6.34 The Find dialog box

3. In the **Find What** field, enter the text you want to search for. You can enter up to 100 characters in this field.

4. Select **Match Case** if you want to match uppercase and lowercase letters exactly.

5. Click on **Find Next** to begin your search. The first occurrence found is highlighted. Continue clicking on **Find Next** to continue your search. To edit the text that is found, select **Close**.

Replacing Text

To replace text:

1. Insert your cursor in a text block.

2. Select **Replace** from the Text menu. The Replace dialog box is displayed, as shown in Figure 6.35.

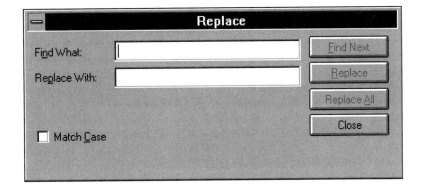

FIGURE 6.35 The Replace dialog box

3. In the **Find What** field, enter the text for which you want to search. You can enter up to 100 characters in this field. In the **Replace With** field, enter the text to replace the Find What text.

4. Select **Match Case** if you want to match uppercase and lowercase letters exactly.

5. Use **Find Next** to search, as you would in the Find dialog box. Select **Replace** to confirm each occurrence of the text that is found. Select **Replace All** to perform a global replace function.

Type Assist

Type Assist provides a number of typing shortcuts to save you time and effort. Select this option from the Text menu, and the Type Assist dialog box, which is shown in Figure 6.36, is displayed.

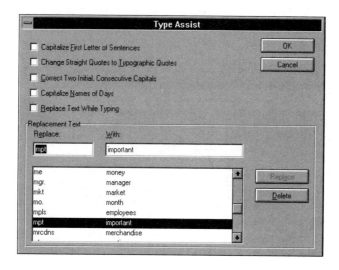

FIGURE 6.36 The Type Assist dialog box

From the Type Assist dialog box, you may perform the following functions:

❖ Automatically capitalize the first letter of each sentence.

❖ Change straight quotes, or ditto marks, to curved typographic quotes.

❖ Automatically correct two initial capital letters.

❖ Automatically capitalize the names of the days of the week.

❖ Use the **Replacement Text** option, allowing you to define shortcuts for words you commonly use—for example, to insert the word *CorelDRAW* automatically when you type the abbreviation, enter **CD** in the **Replace** field and CorelDRAW in the **With** field. Use the Add button to add items to the replacement list. Use the Delete button to remove them. There are a number of preset replacements that come with CorelDRAW.

Print Merge

Print Merge lets you replace text in a drawing with text from a word processor. The advantage to this feature is that your merged text takes on the characteristics (such as font, point size, spacing, and justification) of the text you created with CorelDRAW, but you can easily produce multiple personalized copies. For example, you could create party invitations, as shown in Figure 6.37, and customize them with individualized text.

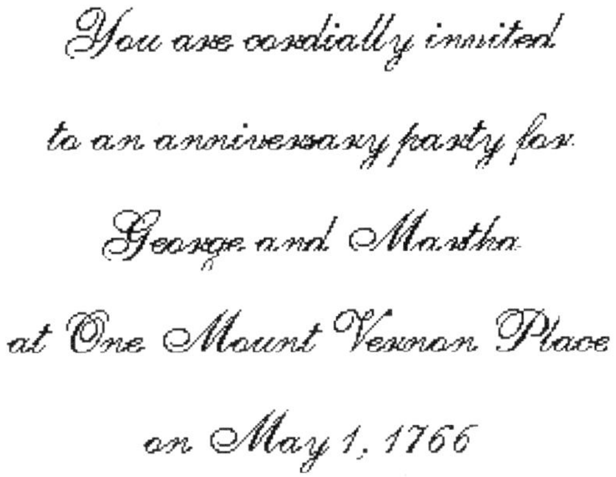

You are cordially invited

to an anniversary party for

George and Martha

at One Mount Vernon Place

on May 1, 1766

FIGURE 6.37 *A party invitation*

The text you merge with your CorelDRAW files must have the following characteristics:

❖ The text must be in an ASCII file, with the file name extension .TXT. Most word processors save files in ASCII format.

❖ The first line of your merge file must indicate the text string to be replaced, which must appear exactly the same way (including any capitalization) as it does in your CorelDRAW graphic, as shown in Figure 6.38. This is called a *primary text string* and is entered in your word processor.

You are cordially invited

to an anniversary party for

NAME 1 and NAME 2

at One Mount Vernon Place

on May 1, 1766

FIGURE 6.38 A party invitation with generic names

❖ In your merge file, each primary text string must be preceded and followed by a backslash (\).

❖ Follow each primary text string by the corresponding *secondary text strings* (the data that will be inserted). They must be in the same sequence as the primary text string and must also be preceded and followed by a backslash (\). The primary and secondary text strings are shown in Figure 6.39.

```
\NAME1\ \NAME2
\JAMES\ \DOLLY
```

FIGURE 6.39 A merge file with primary and secondary text strings

NOTE

Although you can insert as much text as you want, be aware of the space you have allowed in the CorelDRAW graphic to make sure the text fits.

Once your merge file is ready, select **Print Merge** from the File menu and click on the merge text file name in the Print Merge dialog box. This dialog box works in much the same way as the Open dialog box, which enables you to select files.

Once you have chosen your merge file, CorelDRAW automatically displays the appropriate Print Options dialog box to allow you to finish setting up your printout. The final result is displayed in Figure 6.40.

You are cordially invited

to an anniversary party for

James and Dolly

at One Mount Vernon Place

on May 1, 1766

FIGURE 6.40 *The invitation with merged names*

Symbols

In addition to all of the effects that you can create with text, you can also add CorelDRAW symbols to your graphics. The symbol library included with CorelDRAW contains almost 3000 drawings covering a variety of topics ranging from buildings to animals to computers and so on.

To use the symbols, the symbol library files must have been installed when you installed CorelDRAW. If you find that they were not installed, rerun the installation program and copy only the symbol library files to your hard disk.

Select **Symbols Roll-Up** from the Special menu to display the Symbols roll-up menu, which is shown in Figure 6.41. Select the symbol set you want and then click on an individual symbol to select it.

FIGURE 6.41 The Symbols roll-up menu

N O T E

You can also look through the CorelDRAW Symbols and Clip Art catalog to choose the one you want. Note its number and then enter its number in the Symbol # box.

You can specify the symbol size by either typing the size into the box or using the scroll arrows to enlarge or reduce the size value.

Hold the mouse button and drag the symbol onto your page. Modify the symbol just as you would any other curved object in CorelDRAW.

Some symbols are combined (or grouped) objects and must be broken apart for some editing procedures.

Tiling Symbols

Symbols can be tiled to create patterns. Click on **Options** to open the Tile dialog box. Enter the grid size you want and select **OK**.

Summary

Text and symbols are objects and can be modified and manipulated as you would modify or manipulate any other object in CorelDRAW. This chapter covered many different ways to use text, including placing artistic text in a graphic, modifying text, creating and editing paragraph text, using the Text menu and the Text roll-up menu, using the spelling checker and thesaurus to help ensure accuracy of text, using the Shape tool with text, and adding symbols to your graphics.

Chapter 7

Kaleidoscope: Using Color and Color Palettes

CorelDRAW comes with several color palettes including Focoltone colors, Pantone spot colors, Pantone process colors, Trumatch process colors, and a customizable palette. This chapter discusses:

- ❖ Color modeling systems
- ❖ Creating custom colors
- ❖ Using and customizing color palettes

Color Modeling Systems

The existing and custom palettes in CorelDRAW give you the ability to create and use virtually any color that can be represented in print. There are six preset color palettes in CorelDRAW:

❖ A **Uniform** palette created from RGB percentages.

❖ A **Custom** palette that you can change to suit your needs.

❖ A **Focaltone** palette built with process colors created in such a way as to minimize trapping needs.

❖ A **Pantone Spot Color** palette that contains spot colors using the Pantone Matching System (PMS), an exact color-specification model you can use when you need an exact color.

❖ A **Pantone Process Color** palette that specifies process colors using a system similar to the spot color system.

❖ A **Trumatch Process Color** palette that specifies process colors using the Trumatch system.

The palette on the bottom of your screen can be changed by selecting another palette. Open the View menu and select a palette from the Color Palette fly-out menu. Figure 7.1 shows the color palette and the Color Palette menu.

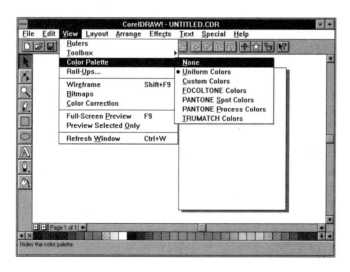

FIGURE 7.1 The color palette and the Color Palette menu

When you create custom colors in CorelDRAW, you can add them to a palette and assign names or numbers to them. You can also delete existing colors or rearrange your palette. You can create a number of different palettes for different projects or clients and save them each under a different name. Custom palettes allow you to work without having to search through existing palettes and allow you to have color consistency among projects or clients.

Color Models

Colors are our perception of different wavelengths of light. Almost all colors can be created by using one of three color-mixing systems, each of which is best suited for a different purpose.

❖ **CMYK** is best suited for representing *reflected colors*—for printing colors. If you have multiple colors, color printing can be expensive because of the need to etch multiple plates. If you are printing more than two colors, you will usually be using process-color printing, which overlays halftones of four different colors—cyan, magenta, yellow, and black (CMYK)—to create an entire range of colors. Cyan, magenta, and yellow are mixed to form the color, black is added to change a color's *tone*. Figure 7.2 shows the CorelDRAW CMYK color selector.

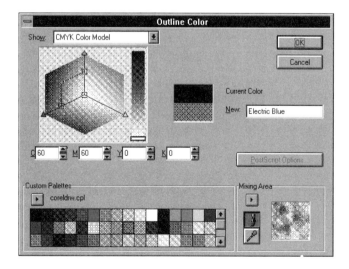

FIGURE 7.2 The CMYK color selector

❖ **RGB** is typically used to create *transmitted colors* and is the method used by color monitors and color televisions. RGB shows colors by using clusters of red, green, and blue phosphors, often referred to as *pixels*. Figure 7.3 shows the CorelDRAW RGB color selector.

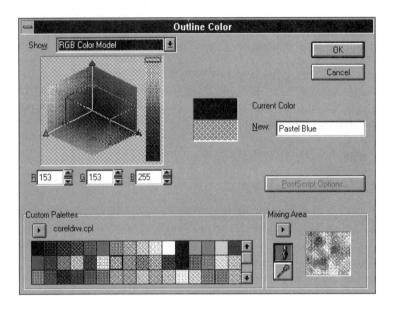

FIGURE 7.3 The RGB color selector

❖ **HSB** relates to the way the human eye perceives color. HSB stands for hue, saturation, and brightness. *Hue* refers to the property of a particular color relating to its frequency, or wavelength, of light. *Saturation* is the extent to which a color is comprised of a selected hue, rather than a combination of that hue and white, as in the difference between red (a heavily saturated color) and pink (a less saturated color). *Brightness* is the degree of lightness or darkness in a color. Figure 7.4 shows the CorelDRAW HSB color selector.

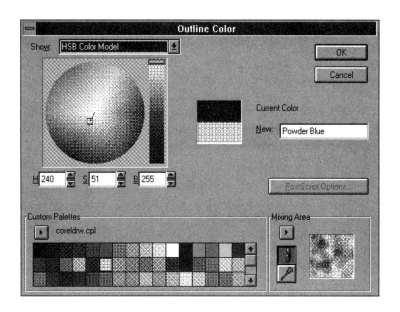

FIGURE 7.4 The HSB color selector

CorelDRAW also has a color selector for grayscale (with 256 levels from which to choose), a handy tool if you are working in black and white.

Spot Color Versus Process Color

Spot color is typically used to add accents to a two-color piece or when exact colors are needed. Any spot color can be tinted to give the illusion of having more colors. A percentage of tint gives your work a lighter shade of the specified color. When you print color separations for a graphic that uses spot color (PostScript printers only), all items that are the same spot color (including tints) print on one plate. Tints are printed as halftones.

Process color refers to the CMYK color model and is used to print most color publications. It is possible to specify over 16 million colors using this model, while having to etch only four plates to print these colors. Process color is typically used when you want to specify more than four colors and when you want to reproduce your piece using a commercial printer.

If you are using a PostScript printer, CorelDRAW can separate your process colors into CMYK plates.

Creating Custom Colors

You can create custom colors by selecting the color wheel icon on either the Outline or Fill tool fly-out menus, which open the Outline Color or Fill Color dialog boxes. Let's create a custom process color in the Outline Color dialog box:

1. Click on the arrow in the Show box to select **CMYK Color Model**.

2. Create the color by adjusting the color selection controls until you find a color you like. If you are using a color reference book, you can enter values in the numeric entry boxes. You may also use the mixing area to see how different colors interact.

SHORTCUT

There can be quite a difference between the color you selected in the book and the way it is displayed on your screen. You can expect your monitor to be inexact when it comes to the display of colors. Even with calibration and a very expensive monitor, color expression on a monitor changes from day to day. This is one of the reasons it is both helpful and advisable to use a color-matching system like Pantone or Trumatch and to keep a color reference book by your computer.

3. Click on **OK** to apply the color to a selected object without adding it to your palette.

4. To add the color to your palette, name the color and press **Enter**.

When you add a color, it is displayed in the Outline Color and Uniform Fill dialog boxes, as well as on the palette on the bottom of your screen.

Using and Customizing Color Palettes

You can open existing palettes and create custom palettes by selecting the color wheel icon on either the Outline or Fill tool fly-out menus. Let's open a palette in the Outline Color dialog box:

1. Click on the Custom Palette button.

2. Select **Open** from the pop-up menu, as shown in Figure 7.5. The Open Palette dialog box is displayed.

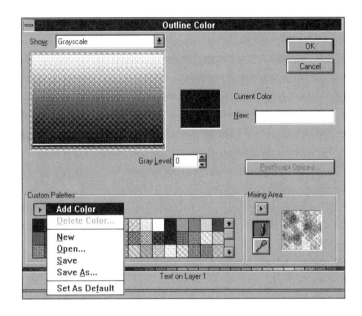

FIGURE 7.5 The Custom Palette pop-up menu

3. Select the name of the palette you want to open and click on **OK**.

Customizing Existing Palettes

You can add, delete, and rearrange colors on any palette. To add a color, select a color, name it in the **Color Name** field, and click on **OK**.

To rearrange colors on an open palette:

1. Click on a color swatch.

2. Drag the color square, represented by a black dot, to its new location in the palette and release the mouse.

N O T E

You cannot add, delete, or rearrange colors on the preset Focaltone, Pantone, or Trumatch palettes. If you would like to customize one of these palettes, select **Save As** from the Custom Palette pop-up menu, rename it, and then make your changes.

To delete colors from a palette, select a color, click on the Custom Palette button, and then select **Delete Color** from the pop-up menu.

To save your palette, click on the Custom Palette button and select **Save**. To change the name of your palette, click on **Save As** and give it a new name.

To create a new palette:

1. Click on the Custom Palette button and select **New**.

2. Choose a color specification method from the show box. Create a new color, name it, click on the Custom Palette button, and select **Add Color** from the pop-up menu.

3. When you have finished building your new palette, save it as described previously.

To specify a palette as the default palette, click on the Custom Palette button and select **Set As Default** from the pop-up menu.

Summary

In this chapter you have gone over some basic color theory and learned about the different types of color models and color-matching systems available in CorelDRAW. You have also learned how to use and customize existing palettes and how to create new palettes.

Chapter 8

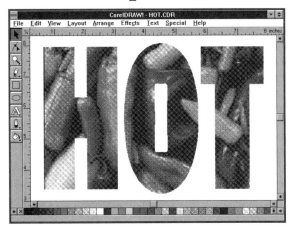

Creating Special Effects

Now that you know how to create and modify shapes with CorelDRAW, you'll probably want to learn how to create all of the exciting effects you see in brochures, magazines, and advertisements.

This chapter covers:

- ❖ Perspective
- ❖ Envelopes
- ❖ Blending objects
- ❖ Extrusion
- ❖ Contouring
- ❖ PowerLines
- ❖ Lenses
- ❖ Powerclips

There are several choices in the Effects menu, which are shown in Figure 8.1, to help you.

Transform Roll-Up	
Clear Transformations	
Add Perspective	
Envelope Roll-Up	Ctrl+F7
Blend Roll-Up	Ctrl+B
Extrude Roll-Up	Ctrl+E
Contour Roll-Up	Ctrl+F9
PowerLine Roll-Up	Ctrl+F8
Lens Roll-Up	Alt+F3
PowerClip	▶
Clear Perspective	
Copy	▶
Clone	▶

FIGURE 8.1 The Effects menu

Perspective

One special effect that is easy to do with CorelDRAW is to apply mathematical perspective to an object. Rather than view an object on a flat plane, you can make one or more of its sides move off in the distance, giving it a feeling of depth.

Adding Perspective to an Object

When you select an object and click on **Add Perspective** from the Effects menu, a dashed box forms around your object, and the tool automatically changes to the Shape tool. This box, however, has four small handles. To see how perspective works, type any word on the screen, as shown in Figure 8.2, and then select the **Perspective** option.

FIGURE 8.2 An item in the perspective box

❖ To show a one-point perspective, move the cursor over one of the handles and drag either horizontally or vertically in the direction you want your object to "vanish."

❖ For a two-point perspective, drag diagonally after you have selected one of the perspective handles.

Figure 8.3 shows one-point perspective added to an object.

FIGURE 8.3 Example of perspective

When you are applying perspectives, you'll see an *X* (two *X*s, if you're using two-point perspective) on your screen in the distance beyond the receding edge of the object. This is called the *vanishing point*, the point at which a line drawn across the top and bottom of the object would eventually meet. You can see the vanishing point only if it is close enough to be in view.

You can also change the perspective after you've applied it by moving the vanishing point. Dragging the *X* handle toward the object lessens the perspective. Dragging it away from the object causes more of the object to disappear from view.

Clear Perspective does not remove the perspective if you add an envelope after you put the object in perspective. Conversely, **Clear Envelope** has no effect if you have since added perspective.

N O T E

Copying Perspective

Perspective can be copied from one object to another. Let's try this by putting another word on the screen. Select the word and choose **Copy Perspective From** from the Copy Effect From pop-up menu. A From arrow is displayed. Move the arrow to the edge of the perspective source and click. Your second word now has the same perspective as the first, as shown in Figure 8.4.

FIGURE 8.4 *A copied perspective*

Even after you put an object in perspective, you can change it. Select your object and then select **Add Perspective** from the Effects menu. CorelDRAW selects the Shape tool and puts the bounding box around the object, so you can change the perspective.

Envelopes

When you work with an *envelope*, your object is placed in one of four modes. Pull on any of the handles of your envelope to distort your object in the direction that you choose.

Applying Envelopes

To illustrate how different envelopes work, let's add an envelope to a word. Open the Effects menu and select **Envelope Roll-up**. The Envelope roll-up menu is displayed, as shown in Figure 8.5.

Press **Ctrl-F7** to open the Envelope roll-up menu.

SHORTCUT

1. Select the object. There are four types of editing envelopes available in CorelDRAW: straight line, single arc, two curves, and unconstrained. Select the left icon, straight line.

FIGURE 8.5 The Envelope roll-up menu

2. Click on **Add New**. A red editing envelope with eight handles appears around the object, as shown in Figure 8.6.

FIGURE 8.6 The editing envelope

NOTE

All initial editing envelopes look the same, regardless of which envelope you select.

3. Click and drag the handle that is in the direction that you want to pull the object. Release the mouse button and click on **Apply**. The object takes on the shape of the modified envelope, as shown in Figure 8.7.

FIGURE 8.7 A straight-line envelope

4. Select **Undo** from the Edit menu to start over.

5. Select **Add New** from the Envelope roll-up menu and select the single-arc envelope (the second icon). When the editing envelope appears, select the same handle as before, and select the object. Notice how different the single-arc envelope looks, as shown in Figure 8.8.

FIGURE 8.8 *A single-arc envelope*

6. Undo your changes again and select **Add New**. This time, select the third icon, or Two Curves mode, and pull the object to see the effects of the envelope, as displayed in Figure 8.9.

FIGURE 8.9 *A two curves envelope*

You can create many different and interesting effects using the two-curves envelope. You can pull the arcs upward, downward, or side-to-side; you can even get a twisted effect, as shown in Figure 8.10.

FIGURE 8.10 *Three examples of using a two-curves envelope*

If you like, you can apply an unconstrained envelope, using the fourth icon. In this mode you can select more than one of the handles (using either the **Shift** key when you click or the marquee-select method before you click) and pull them. Unlike the first three envelopes, the unconstrained envelope nodes have control points that can be manipulated for further control. This, too, can give some interesting results, as shown in Figure 8.11.

FIGURE 8.11 *An unconstrained envelope*

You can use one of CorelDRAW's preset envelope shapes to create an envelope:

1. Select an object.
2. Click on **Add Preset**.
3. Select an envelope shape.
4. Click on **Apply** to apply your change.

Copying Envelopes

Once you have achieved an envelope style you like, you can copy it to another object. Do this using the Effects menu, as you did with Perspective, or you can use the **Create From** option on the Envelope roll-up menu.

Mapping Options

The Envelope roll-up menu has several mapping options available from the drop-down menu on the middle of the Envelope roll-up menu. *Mapping* affects the distortion of an object. There are five mapping options:

❖ **Original** is the mode used by envelopes in the previous version of CorelDRAW (4.0). If you are importing files from version 4.0, use this option so that envelopes created in version 4.0 do not loose their shape.

❖ **Putty** produces less exaggerated distortions than Original mode, basing the shape on the corner nodes only.

❖ **Vertical** fits objects to envelopes by distorting them from the top and bottom. It is most suited to vertically oriented objects, such as text. Figure 8.12 shows text with Original mode and Vertical mode envelopes.

FIGURE 8.12 Text with Original mode and Vertical mode envelopes

❖ **Horizontal** fits objects to envelopes by distorting them from their sides. Horizontal mode helps to maintain the horizontal integrity of objects. Figure 8.13 shows an object with Original mode and Horizontal mode envelopes.

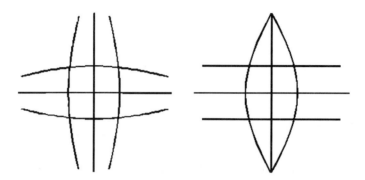

FIGURE 8.13 Objects with Original mode and Horizontal mode envelopes

❖ **Text** is applied to paragraph text that you want to shape. When you select a paragraph, CorelDRAW automatically selects this mode.

Check **Keep Lines** to keep straight lines straight, or CorelDRAW adjusts them with the envelope, as shown in Figure 8.14. Select **Reset Envelope** to remove all envelopes applied to an object.

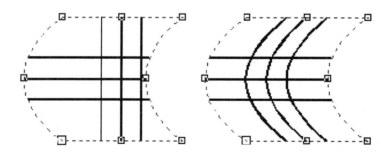

FIGURE 8.14 An object with Keep Lines selected and one without

Blending Objects

Blending objects makes one object seem to melt into another. As the objects blend, the outline, fill, size, and shape of the first object are transformed to the outline, fill, size, and shape of the second object. CorelDRAW creates all the shapes or steps along the way, creating a smooth transition from the first object to the second.

Applying a Blend

To illustrate blending, create two objects, a black rectangle and a white ellipse. Select the objects, then select **Blend Roll-Up** from the Effects menu. The Blend roll-up menu is displayed, as shown in Figure 8.15.

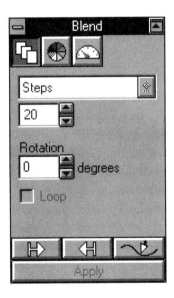

FIGURE 8.15 The Blend roll-up menu

Using the default values shown, click on **Apply**, and the objects are blended, as shown in Figure 8.16. The number of steps specified in this example is 20. This indicates how many intermediate shapes CorelDRAW creates to blend the objects. A greater number of steps creates a more gradual transformation, as displayed in Figure 8.17.

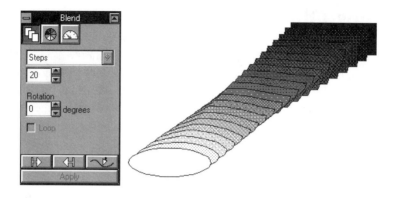

FIGURE 8.16 *A blended rectangle and ellipse*

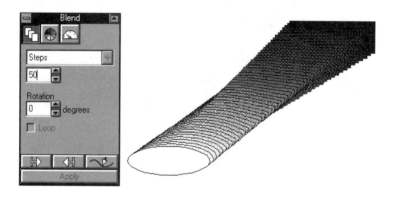

FIGURE 8.17 *A blended rectangle and ellipse with 50 steps*

Fewer steps cause a sharper gradation between the two objects. Fewer steps also result in a greater distance between the blended objects, and more steps yield a smaller distance between the intermediate objects.

Changing Rotation

You can also change the appearance of your blend by changing the rotation. All of the examples we just looked at showed a 0° rotation, which gives you a straight line from point A to point B (or in our case, from the ellipse to the rectangle). By entering a number in the **Rotation** box, you can change the slope of the rotation. Watch what happens when you rotate the blend 45°, as shown in Figure 8.18.

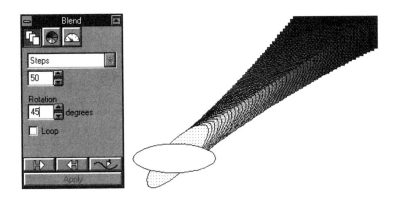

FIGURE 8.18 *A blend rotated 45°*

Placing a Blend on a Path

You can also place a blend on a designated path. In this example, we'll create a curved path for the blend, as shown in Figure 8.19.

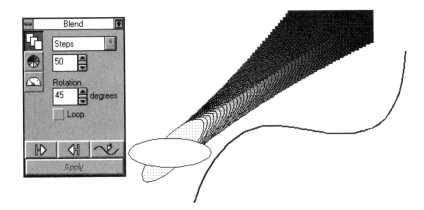

FIGURE 8.19 *A blend with a curve*

1. Create the path you want your blend to follow.

2. With the Blend roll-up menu on the screen, make sure the objects you want to blend are selected.

3. Click on the picture of the curve in the Blend roll-up menu. Choose **New Path** from the submenu. A small hooked arrow is displayed.

4. Place the arrow on the curve and click.

5. Click on **Apply**, and the blend is placed on the curve that you selected, as shown in Figure 8.20.

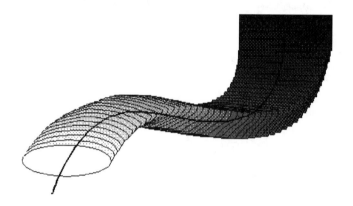

FIGURE 8.20 A blend following a Bézier curve

Options on the path submenu allow you to highlight your path (**Show Path**) or remove the blend from its path (**Detach from Path**).

Other Blend Options

You can also change the colors in your blend or set the start and end objects in your blend from the Blend roll-up menu.

To change the order of the blend, in other words, to place the black rectangle on the top and the white ellipse on the bottom, open the Arrange menu and select **Reverse Order** from the Order pop-up menu.

You can also work with individual items within the blend. Make sure that the blend is selected and select **Separate** from the Arrange menu. A node appears on each of the objects, allowing you to move or shape the individual items.

Click on the Rainbow Colorwheel icon to specify how colors are blended. If you select **Rainbow**, CorelDRAW chooses the intermediate colors from a path around the colorwheel. The rotation buttons below the **Rainbow** option let you specify the direction the colors rotate.

Extrusion

When you extrude an object, CorelDRAW draws in some of the surfaces that illustrate that object's third dimension.

Applying Extrusion

Draw a rectangle and select **Extrude Roll-up** from the Effects menu. The Extrude roll-up menu, as shown in Figure 8.21, appears.

FIGURE 8.21 The Extrude roll-up menu

Press **Ctrl-E** to open the Extrude roll-up menu.

With the defaults selected, click on **Apply**, and the rectangle appears with the extrusion lines and effects shown in Figure 8.22. CorelDRAW comes with over 40 preset extrusion effects.

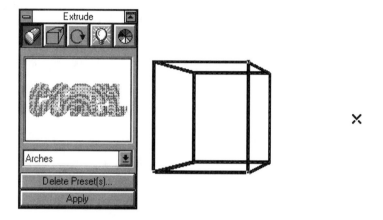

FIGURE 8.22 A rectangle with the extrusion applied

Adding Perspective

The first and second icons on the Extrude roll-up menu create prespective in an extruded object. If you choose the second icon, CorelDRAW displays a depth box that allows you to specify the depth of the extrusion, as shown in Figure 8.23.

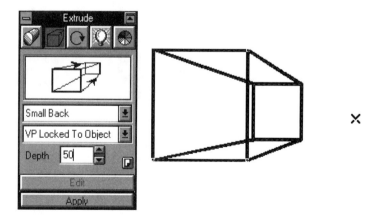

FIGURE 8.23 An extruded rectangle with a depth of 50

A depth of 99 extends the extrusion all the way to the vanishing point. A depth of -99 extends the extrusion as far as possible away from the vanishing point.

You can apply extrusion to objects that are already in perspective.

N O T E

Changing Orientation

You can also change the orientation of your extruded object. The third icon on the Extrude roll-up menu (the circle with the arrow) controls spatial orientation. If you click on this option, a three-dimensional sphere is displayed in the window in the roll-up menu, with three bands running horizontally and vertically across the sphere and around the circumference of the sphere.

If you click on one of the arrows on the horizontal diameter, the object is shifted to the left or right. Figure 8.24 shows the rectangle with a right orientation.

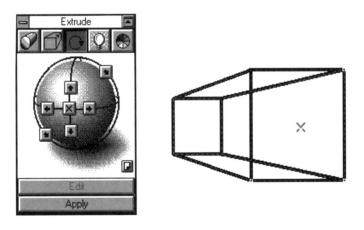

FIGURE 8.24 *An extruded rectangle with a right orientation*

Clicking on one of the vertical diameter arrows changes the orientation upward or downward. If you click on one of the arrows around the circumference, the orientation changes in a clockwise or counterclockwise direction.

Adding a Light Source

To add a shaded effect to your extrusion, adjust the hypothetical light source.

1. Choose the fourth icon, the lightbulb, from the top of the Extrude roll-up menu.

2. Select an intensity from one of the three lightbulbs on the left, and a shaded sphere is displayed in the center of a wireframe cube.

3. To locate the light source, click on any point on the wireframe where two lines meet and then click on **Apply**. Figure 8.25 shows the effects of changing the light source.

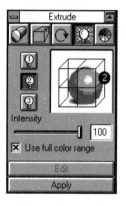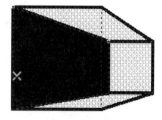

FIGURE 8.25 An extruded rectangle with a light source

Changing Color

By selecting the last icon, the colorwheel, on the Extrude roll-up menu, you can also change the color of the extrusion.

Practice Session

Although the envelope, perspective, blend, and extrude options give interesting results individually, you can combine these options to maximize your effects, as illustrated by the following example:

1. Put a word on the screen, place it in an envelope, and manipulate it.
2. Add perspective, as shown in Figure 8.26.

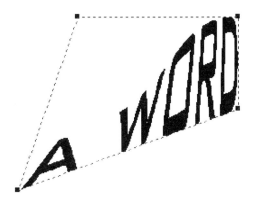

FIGURE 8.26 A word in an envelope and with perspective added

3. Put another word on the screen. Select it and choose **Copy Envelope From** from the Effects menu, place the arrow on the second object, and click on **Envelopes**.
4. Select both objects, open the Blend roll-up menu, and then click on **Apply**. Figure 8.27 shows the result of the blend.

FIGURE 8.27 Blended objects

Contouring

Contouring is similar to blending, however, *contouring* applies to one object, whereas *blending* applies to two objects. Contours can be applied to the inside, outside, or center of an object.

 Contours cannot be applied to bitmapped objects, grouped objects, or OLE objects.

N O T E

Applying a Contour

Select **Contour Roll-Up** from the Effects menu. The Contour roll-up menu is shown in Figure 8.28.

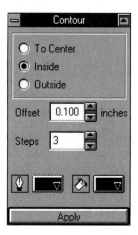

FIGURE 8.28 The Contour roll-up menu

 Press **Ctrl-F9** to open the Contour roll-up menu.

SHORTCUT

To contour an object:

1. Place an object on the screen.

2. Click on one of the orientation options to select the direction your contour will take: **To Center**, **Inside**, or **Outside**.

3. Enter the offset distance for the steps of the contour.

4. Enter the number of steps you want the contour to take.

5. Choose colors for both your outline and fill and then select **Apply** to apply the contour to your object. Figure 8.29 shows contouring applied to the center, inside, and outside of an object.

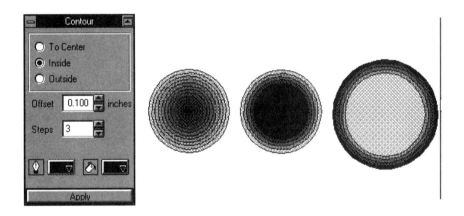

FIGURE 8.29 Contouring applied to the center, inside, and outside of an object

PowerLines

PowerLines give your graphics a hand-drawn look by applying variable weights to lines, as if you were using a pressure-sensitive graphics tablet. The resulting effects include tapered, etched, calligraphic, and hand-drawn lines.

Open the Effects menu and select **PowerLine Roll-Up**, as shown in Figure 8.30.

FIGURE 8.30 The PowerLine roll-up menu

There are three option icons in the upper-left corner of the Powerline roll-up menu:

❖ **Preset PowerLines**. There are 23 preset PowerLine tools. The **Pressure** option may be used with pressure-sensitive pen tablets. Select an object, choose a preset option, set the maximum width to the desired level, and then click on **Apply**. Figure 8.31 shows a few of the preset options.

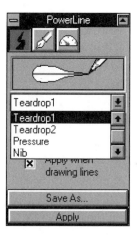

FIGURE 8.31 Some PowerLine Preset options

❖ **Nib Shape**. Click on the Page toggle icon to select the Nib Angle, Nib Ratio, and Intensity. You can add a new nib to the Preset menu by clicking on **Save As**, giving the new nib a name, and clicking on **OK**. Figure 8.32 shows a nib shape option.

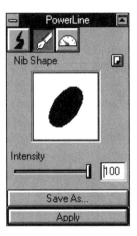

FIGURE 8.32 Nib Shape options

❖ **Image controls**. Set your speed, spread, and ink flow by entering the desired values in the numeric boxes or use the slide bars. Select **Scale with Image** to resize PowerLines without losing your original values. The image controls are shown in Figure 8.33.

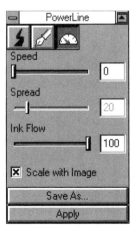

FIGURE 8.33 PowerLine image controls

To edit the nodes of your PowerLines:

1.   Draw a Bézier curve, select the **Bullet2** PowerLine, and click on **Apply**.

2.   Select the object with the Shape tool, and a core line is displayed, as shown in Figure 8.34.

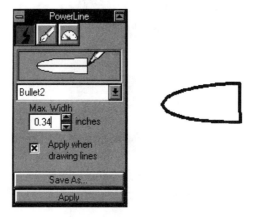

FIGURE 8.34 A core line

3.   Double-click on one of the nodes of the core line to display the Node Edit roll-up menu.

4.   Click on **Pressure Edit** in the Node Edit roll-up menu.

5.   Click and drag the pressure-edit handles to reshape your PowerLine, as shown in Figure 8.35.

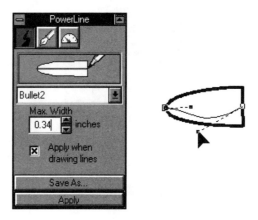

FIGURE 8.35 Reshaping a PowerLine

Lenses

You can apply one of eight lenses to objects that have closed paths. You can apply a lens to a group of objects, but you cannot group objects that have lenses applied. (Got that?)

Open the Effects menu and select **Lens Roll-Up**. The Lens roll-up menu, which is shown in Figure 8.36, appears.

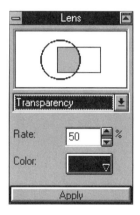

FIGURE 8.36 The Lens roll-up menu

To use a lens, select an object and then select the type of lens you want to apply. Figure 8.37 shows an inverted lens applied to an object.

FIGURE 8.37 An inverted lens applied to a lion

Powerclips

A *powerclip* places one object inside another, giving a cut-out effect.

With powerclips, the *containter object* houses the *contents object*. You may have up to five levels of contents in a containter.

For example, you can take a square photograph (contents) and place it into a star-shaped container, and the photograph is clipped to fit the star.

To use a powerclip, select the contents and then choose **Place Inside Container** from the Powerclip fly-out menu in the Effects menu. A large black arrow is displayed. Use this arrow to select the container for your object, as shown in Figure 8.38. Figure 8.39 shows the results of this powerclip.

FIGURE 8.38 *Using a powerclip*

FIGURE 8.39 *An image placed in a container*

FIGURE 1

The original photograph, left, and the same photograph after the application of CorelPHOTO-PAINT's Pointillism filter.

FIGURE 2

The same original photo-graph shown in Figure 1 using CorelPHOTO-PAINT's Impressionism filter.

FIGURE 3

The same original photo-graph shown in Figure 1 using CorelPHOTO-PAINT's Edge Detect filter.

FIGURE 4

The same original photo-graph shown in Figure 1 using CorelPHOTO-PAINT's Invert filter.

FIGURE 5

The original photograph, left, and the same photograph after the application of CorelPHOTO-PAINT's Contour filter.

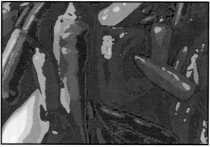

FIGURE 6

The same original photo-graph shown in Figure 5 using CorelPHOTO-PAINT's Posterize filter.

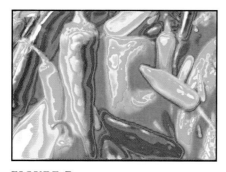

FIGURE 7

The same original photograph shown in Figure 5 using CorelPHOTO-PAINT's Psychedelic filter.

FIGURE 8

The same original photograph shown in Figure 5 using CorelPHOTO-PAINT's Solarize filter.

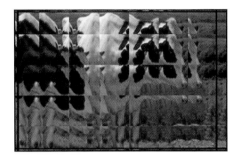

FIGURE 9

The original photograph, left, and the same photograph after the application of CorelPHOTO-PAINT's Glass Block filter.

FIGURE 10

The same original photograph shown in Figure 9 using CorelPHOTO-PAINT's Impressionist Mapping filter.

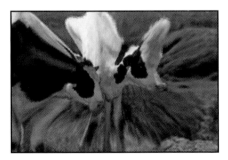

FIGURE 11

The same original photograph shown in Figure 9 using CorelPHOTO-PAINT's Pinch/Punch filter.

FIGURE 12

The same original photo-graph shown in Figure 9 using CorelPHOTO-PAINT's Pixelate filter.

FIGURE 13

The original photograph, left, and the same photograph after the application of CorelPHOTO-PAINT's Ripple filter.

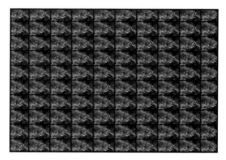

FIGURE 14

The same original photograph shown in Figure 13 using CorelPHOTO-PAINT's Tile filter.

FIGURE 15

The same original photograph shown in Figure 13 using CorelPHOTO-PAINT's Vignette filter.

FIGURE 16

The same original photograph shown in Figure 13 using CorelPHOTO-PAINT's Wind filter.

Summary

In this chapter you learned how to use the options on the Effects menu to add some exciting effects, including shaping an object with different types of envelopes, putting an object in perspective to give it a feeling of depth, blending several objects along a path, and managing the steps in the blend. You also learned how to create three-dimensional effects using extrusion, how to apply contouring to an object, how to use PowerLines and lenses, and how to place objects in containers using the powerclip feature.

Chapter 9

Aiding and Abetting: CorelMOSAIC

As you work with the different Corel applications, you'll begin to appreciate the difficulty of keeping track of the many graphics files you create.

CorelMOSAIC displays a list of all of the files available to you and also gives you a visual preview of your graphics files. Using CorelMOSAIC, you can select a number of files and then perform certain CorelDRAW functions on them. In addition, CorelMOSAIC includes a collection function that compresses your images to conserve your disk space. The CorelMOSAIC collection allows you to reorganize your graphics, even if they reside in different directories. CorelMOSAIC's catalog feature allows you to create groups of images that do not necessarily have to be in the same directory. CorelMOSAIC also has a keyword indexing function for large volumes of files. This chapter covers:

❖ File management functions

❖ Libraries

❖ Printing files in batches

❖ Selecting, locating, or finding file information

When you open CorelMOSAIC, an almost blank screen area is displayed with only four items on the menu bar—File, Edit, Window, and Help.

File Management Functions

When files are placed in *libraries*, they are automatically compressed. When a library is opened in CorelMOSAIC, *thumbnails*—small representations of the file—are displayed. CorelMOSAIC also views and converts files from a Photo CD disk.

To compress your files on disk and conserve disk space, you can store your files in a library. Each library consists of two files, a *.CLB file and a *.CLH file. Be sure both files are present if you move or otherwise manipulate your files on disk. Once you have created the library files, you can delete the original CorelDRAW files from disk.

WARNING

Test library files by expanding them and make sure all your files are there before you delete the *.CDR files.

A library also allows you to reorganize your files in a different way than they are organized in your directories, because your library can consist of files from several different directories.

To begin working with CorelMOSAIC, open the File menu, which is shown in Figure 9.1.

FIGURE 9.1 The CorelMOSAIC File menu

Viewing a Library

To view a collection of images, select **Open Collection** from the File menu. The Open Collection dialog box is shown in Figure 9.2.

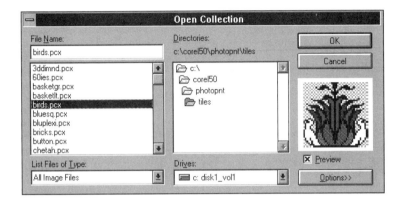

FIGURE 9.2 The Open Collection dialog box

Select the drive and directory you want to view. Let's select **c:\corel50\photopnt\tiles**. Click on **OK**, and the entire graphic contents of the directory is displayed, as shown in Figure 9.3. Keep this window open for the next exercise.

FIGURE 9.3 The graphic contents of the Tiles subdirectory

Libraries

You have a new client who is in the masonry business. You need an available library of brick images to create the graphics. The existing tiles collection contains a good selection for starters.

To create a new masonry library:

1. Select **New Collection** from the File menu. The Create New Collection dialog box is shown in Figure 9.4.

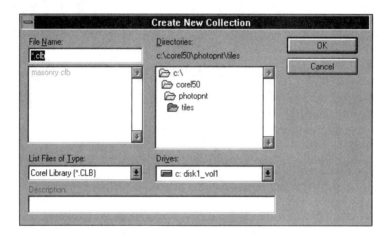

FIGURE 9.4 The Create New Collection dialog box

2. Enter **masonry** in the **File Name** field, select the directory in which you want it saved, and click on **OK**. CorelMOSAIC opens an empty window with the name of your file on the title bar.

3. Click on the thumbnail of the bricks (**bricks.pcx**) and drag it from the tiles window to the masonry window. As you drag, a page icon is displayed informing you that you are copying a graphic. Figure 9.5 shows the copying process.

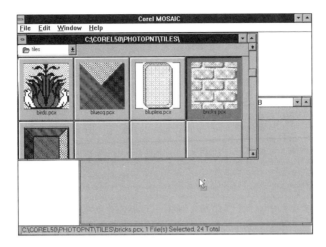

FIGURE 9.5 Copying a thumbnail

4. If you are asked to confirm your copy action, select **Yes**.

5. Continue adding all of the masonry-like graphics to your new library, which is shown in Figure 9.6.

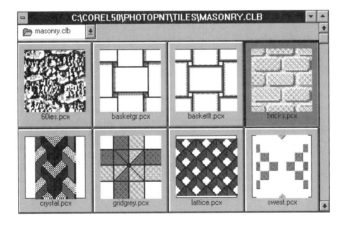

FIGURE 9.6 The new masonry library

You can use this click-and-drag method to add files to any library or catalog.

Opening a Library

To open an existing library, select **Open Collection** from the File menu. When the Open Collection dialog box is displayed, select the library or catalog from the appropriate directory.

Deleting a Library

To remove a library from your disk permanently, select **Delete Collection** from the File menu. Select the library you would like to delete from the appropriate directory and then select **OK**. Choose **Yes** to confirm your deletion.

Printing Files in Batches

You can print one or more files from a CorelMOSAIC library as a batch operation:

1. Select the files you want to print. To select multiple files, hold down the **Ctrl** key while clicking on the thumbnails.

2. Choose **Print Files** from the File menu. CorelMOSAIC must expand the compressed files before it can print them. The Directory To Expand Files To dialog box is shown in Figure 9.7.

3. Select a directory in which to place the expanded files from the Directory To Expand Files To and then select **OK**. CorelDRAW is opened and loads each file you selected.

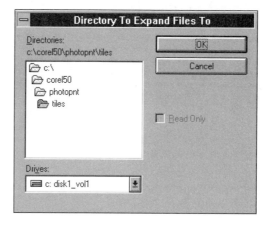

FIGURE 9.7 The Directory To Expand Files To dialog box

4. Choose your print specifications for each file and select **OK**.

You can also print the thumbnails that are displayed in CorelMOSAIC by selecting the thumbnails you want to print and choosing **Print Thumbnails** from the File menu. Select your printing specifications and click on **OK**.

In the Preferences dialog box, which is shown in Figure 9.8, you can select the thumbnail display, as well as the width and height of the thumbnails. Open this dialog box by selecting **Preferences** from the File menu.

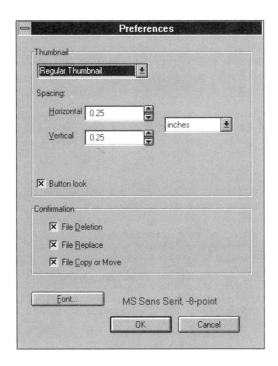

FIGURE 9.8 The Preferences dialog box

You can also change the font and size of the label. Click on **Font** to display the Font dialog box. Select your font attributes and click on **OK**.

You can also choose to display confirmation messages for deleting, replacing, and copying or moving files.

Selecting **Text Only** from the Thumbnail drop-down list box displays file names and associated information instead of thumbnails, as shown in Figure 9.9.

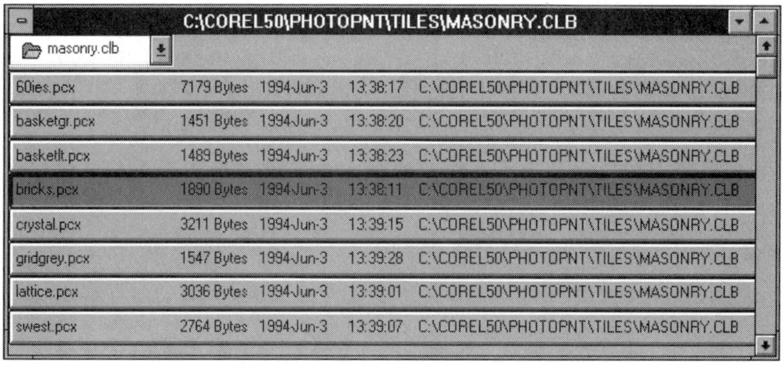
C:\COREL50\PHOTOPNT\TILES\MASONRY.CLB
masonry.clb
60ies.pcx 7179 Bytes 1994-Jun-3 13:38:17 C:\COREL50\PHOTOPNT\TILES\MASONRY.CLB
basketgr.pcx 1451 Bytes 1994-Jun-3 13:38:20 C:\COREL50\PHOTOPNT\TILES\MASONRY.CLB
basketlt.pcx 1489 Bytes 1994-Jun-3 13:38:23 C:\COREL50\PHOTOPNT\TILES\MASONRY.CLB
bricks.pcx 1890 Bytes 1994-Jun-3 13:38:11 C:\COREL50\PHOTOPNT\TILES\MASONRY.CLB
crystal.pcx 3211 Bytes 1994-Jun-3 13:39:15 C:\COREL50\PHOTOPNT\TILES\MASONRY.CLB
gridgrey.pcx 1547 Bytes 1994-Jun-3 13:39:28 C:\COREL50\PHOTOPNT\TILES\MASONRY.CLB
lattice.pcx 3036 Bytes 1994-Jun-3 13:39:01 C:\COREL50\PHOTOPNT\TILES\MASONRY.CLB
swest.pcx 2764 Bytes 1994-Jun-3 13:39:07 C:\COREL50\PHOTOPNT\TILES\MASONRY.CLB

FIGURE 9.9 Displaying a library in Text Only mode

Selecting, Locating, or Finding File Information

You can use the CorelMOSAIC Edit menu, which is shown in Figure 9.10, to select or deselect files, import and export files to and from CorelDRAW, examine file information, work with keywords, and merge text back into files.

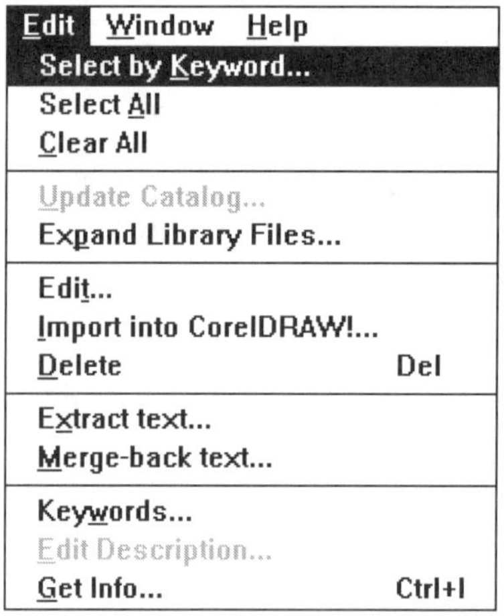
Edit Window Help
Select by Keyword...
Select All
Clear All
Update Catalog...
Expand Library Files...
Edit...
Import into CorelDRAW!...
Delete Del
Extract text...
Merge-back text...
Keywords...
Edit Description...
Get Info... Ctrl+I

FIGURE 9.10 The Edit menu

The following options are in the Edit menu:

- ❖ **Select by Keyword** uses keyword information that you assign when you save the files in CorelDRAW. This option selects files based on those keywords.

- ❖ **Select All** selects all files whose thumbnails appear on the screen.

- ❖ **Clear All** deselects any files that are currently selected.

- ❖ **Edit** opens either a *.CDR file into CorelDRAW, a *.PCX file into CorelPHOTO-PAINT, or a *.SHW file into CorelSHOW so that you can edit it.

- ❖ **Import into CorelDRAW** is similar to using the **Edit** option on a *.CDR file. It opens the CorelDRAW application and displays the drawing on your screen.

- ❖ **Export into CorelDRAW** opens the Export dialog box and allows you to choose the type of file you want to export.

- ❖ **Delete** removes the selected file from the specified library or directory. If you check **Confirm** on the File Deletion check box, CorelMOSAIC prompts you for confirmation before deleting a file.

- ❖ **Extract text** transfers text from CorelDRAW graphics into ASCII format for editing in a word processing application.

- ❖ **Merge-back text** brings a merged text file into CorelDRAW.

- ❖ **Keywords** displays the Keyword Search dialog box, which is shown in Figure 9.11, and allows keywords associated with the selected catalog or library file.

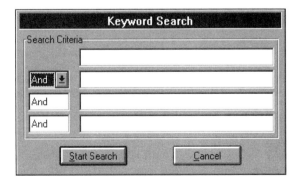

FIGURE 9.11 The Keyword Search dialog box

❖ **Get Info** displays the File Information dialog box, which is shown in Figure 9.12. It includes information about the currently selected file, such as its size in bytes.

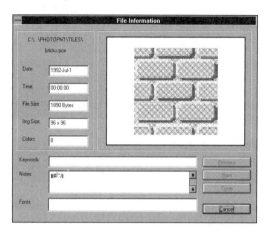

FIGURE 9.12 The File Information dialog box

Expanding Library Files

Once you select your library, you can expand files from it. Select the files you want and choose **Expand Library Files** from the Edit menu. The Directory To Extract Files To dialog box, which is shown in Figure 9.13, is displayed.

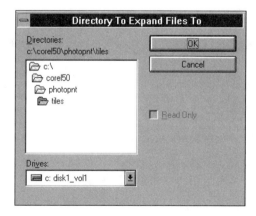

FIGURE 9.13 The Directory To Extract Files To dialog box

Once the files are expanded, you can choose any other CorelMOSAIC option, such as **Print** or **Import**, and CorelMOSAIC processes the expanded files sequentially.

NOTE

CorelDRAW cannot open or print compressed files. You must first expand them with CorelMOSAIC.

Summary

In this chapter you learned how to use CorelMOSAIC to organize your files. To help you find the files you need, CorelMOSAIC lets you select from thumbnails, which are the small representations of your graphics files. Once you select one or more of CorelMOSAIC's thumbnails, you can perform a variety of different functions, such as printing files or thumbnails of files and selecting files using keywords. CorelMOSAIC also contains a library function that compresses graphics files and creates libraries.

Chapter 10

Stay Within the Lines: CorelTRACE

This chapter covers how to use CorelTRACE to edit scanned images and other bitmapped graphics to create better graphics. After you traced the scanned images, you can use them in other applications, and since they are now vector graphics, you can take advantage of your printer's highest resolutions. This chapter covers:

- ❖ How CorelTRACE works
- ❖ Importing images
- ❖ Tracing images
- ❖ CorelTRACE tips and tricks

How CorelTRACE Works

CorelTRACE traces a variety of bitmapped image types to create vector graphics, giving you smooth lines and curves as well as the kind of resolution that takes advantage of high-resolution printers. Tracing your image also produces graphics files that occupy far less disk space than the original images. You can use this program for many different types of images including technical illustrations, architectural drawings, logos, and letterheads. CorelTRACE replicates colors and shades of gray so you can reproduce an image that looms close to the original.

Once you trace your image, you can import it into CorelDRAW or CorelPHOTO-PAINT for some additional touch-up work. However, you can also import the traced image directly into other applications, such as CorelVentura, PageMaker, WordPerfect, Microsoft Word, Ami Pro, and Arts and Letters.

Starting CorelTRACE

Begin CorelTRACE the same way you do any of the other applications in the CorelDRAW Program Manager group. Simply double-click on its icon, and the CorelTRACE screen, which is shown in Figure 10.1, is displayed.

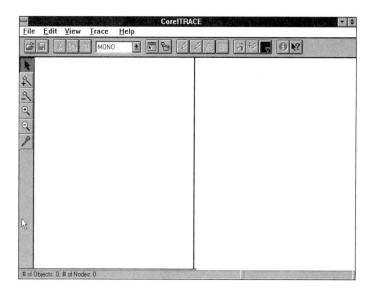

FIGURE 10.1 The CorelTRACE screen

Under the menu bar is a button bar that has shortcuts for many menu selections. Use the drop-down menu to select the mode for your trace: Color, Dithered, Form, or Monochrome.

Along the left of your screen is a toolbox with the following elements:

❖ A **Pick tool** that allows you to use the marquee-select method on areas of a source document.

❖ Two **Magic Wand tools** to select and deselect color areas.

❖ Two **Zoom tools** to increase and decrease viewing magnification.

❖ An **Eyedropper tool** to pick up colors from existing images.

Importing Images

The acceptable file formats for importing images are shown in Table 10.1.

TABLE 10.1 Importing Different File Images

Application	File Format
CompuServe bitmap	*.GIF
JPEG bitmap	*.JPG, *.JFF, *.JTF, *.CMP
Kodak Photo CD Image	*.PCD
Paintbrush	*.PCX
Scitex CT bitmap	*.SCT, *.CT
Targa bitmap	*.TGA, *,VDA, *.ICB, *.VST
TIFF bitmap	*.TIF, *.SEP, *.CPT
Windows bitmap	*.BMP, *.DIB, *.RLE

To import an image into CorelTRACE, select **Open** from the File menu. The Open dialog box, which is shown in Figure 10.2, is displayed.

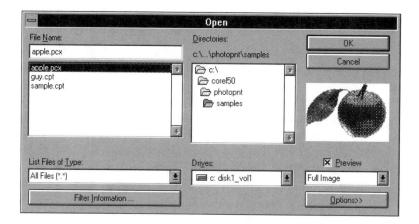

FIGURE 10.2 The Open dialog box

In the **List Files of Type** field, be sure you have selected the type of file you want to import. Also, check the Drives and Directories boxes to make sure that you are addressing the drive and directory where your bitmap files are located. Select a bitmap and click on **OK**.

What to Trace

Before we go on, let's talk a little bit about what makes a good candidate for tracing. High-contrast images make good candidates. Black-and-white line art also traces well. If you'll be tracing color images, those with solid colors trace better than those with shaded color areas. You can also get good results with grayscale images, which are made up of several shades of gray.

Choose artwork that is clear and sharp—make sure you scan it at the highest possible resolution. Fine-tune using the contrast and intensity settings on your scanner to get the best results.

You can use a higher resolution with black-and-white images than with grayscale or color images. Scanning color and grayscale images at higher resolutions produces very large disk files without much real improvement in image quality.

You may want to enlarge, or scale, very small images to make them easier to trace. Be careful, however, not to magnify an image more than 300%, because that can result in a loss of quality. Conversely, try not to scan overly large images. You can reduce image size by including only the portions you wish to trace and by cropping unused white space in the image.

Tracing Methods and Options

Once you've opened an image in CorelTRACE, set your output options and tracing options before beginning the trace.

Tracing Methods

You must also decide how your trace will be done before you actually trace the image you selected. Click on the Trace menu, which is shown in Figure 10.3.

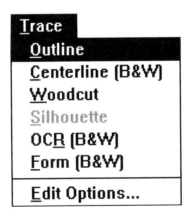

FIGURE 10.3 The Trace menu

Outline

Outline traces the edges of each element, filling in the closed areas of each element with the appropriate color. For example, if you're tracing an image in black-and-white, the original colors are preserved in the traced image. For color or grayscale traced images, CorelTRACE selects the colors that come closest to the original.

Use the outline method for tracing images that consist mostly of thick, filled objects.

Centerline (B&W)

When you choose the **Centerline** method, CorelTRACE enables you to trace along the center of lines and curves in an object, but not along its outline. Images that are thick and filled are traced like the **Outline** method. This method works best with images that consist of many thin, black lines. Images must be in black and white before you can trace it using the **Centerline** option.

Woodcut

The **Woodcut** method create a traced image that has lines drawn across it in angles.

Silhouette

Silhouette traces the outline of an object and fills it in with a single specified color.

OCR (B&W)

OCR converts scanned text into vector graphics that you can manipulate in CorelDRAW.

Form (B&W)

The **Form** option traces text, lines, and objects in a black-and-white format.

Tracing Options

You can modify the standard settings for tracing methods by selecting **Edit Options** from the Trace menu. Select a method to modify from tabs in the Tracing Options dialog box.

Use the Setting area at the bottom of the dialog box to set defaults for each of the tracing modes (Color, Dithered, Form, and Monochrome).

Image

Image controls how the source image will be traced. The Image tab is shown in Figure 10.4.

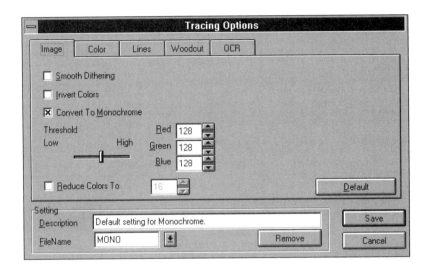

FIGURE 10.4 The Image tab

❖ **Smooth Dithering** smoothes jagged pixels to improve the traced image.

❖ **Invert Colors** inverts the RGB value of colors.

❖ **Convert To Monochrome** converts color images (using RGB values) to black-and-white images.

❖ **Threshold** controls the contrast of RGB values when converting to monochrome. **Convert To Monochrome** must be selected to use this function.

❖ **Reduce Colors To** automatically reduces the number of colors in the bitmap.

Color

The Color tab, which is shown in Figure 10.5, controls the color tolerance value.

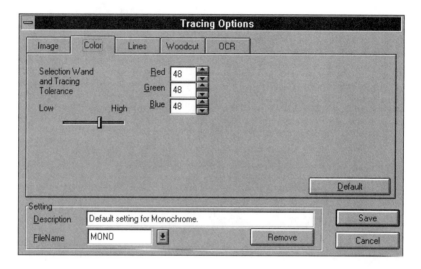

FIGURE 10.5 The Color tab

A low value on the slide bar closely matches colors. A high value means that traced colors must be in the same color range.

Lines

The Lines tab, which is shown in Figure 10.6, controls the tracing parameters for the **Outline** and **Centerline** tracing methods.

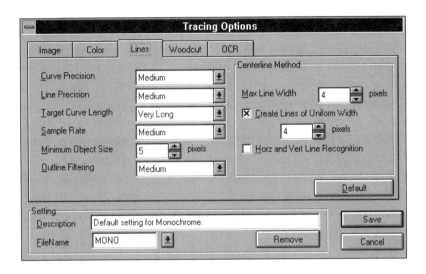

FIGURE 10.6 The Lines tab

❖ **Curve Precision** indicates how precise the trace should be when following a line in the original image.

❖ **Line Precision** controls the amount of detail captured. The default setting captures a maximum amount of detail.

❖ **Target Curve Length** limits the length of individual curves. A shorter curve length produces more detail than a long one.

❖ **Sample Rate** controls the averaging of points in a graphic. Select a fine rate for a close match and a coarser rate for a less exact match.

❖ **Minimum Object Size** counts the number of pixels in an object's outline. Specify a low value to increase the detail in a traced image or a high value to reduce the detail.

The Centerline Method area controls the tracing parameters for the Centerline tracing method.

❖ **Max Line Width** specifies the widest object that will be used as a centerline in a trace.

❖ **Create Line of Uniform Width** assigns a specific weight to all lines in the image. You can specify from 1 to 50 pixels.

❖ **Horz and Vert Line Recognition** outputs an image with perfectly horizontal and vertical lines.

Woodcut

The Woodcut tab, which is shown in Figure 10.7, controls the tracing parameters for the Woodcut Style tracing method.

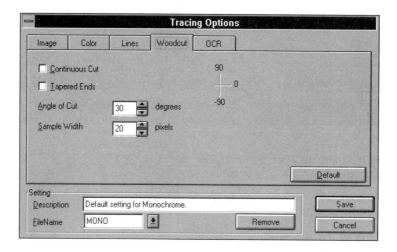

FIGURE 10.7 The Woodcut tab

❖ **Continuous Cut** generates a cut without breaks.

❖ **Tapered Ends** produces a gradual narrowing effect for line ends.

❖ **Angle of Cut** specifies line angles.

❖ **Sample Width** specifies, in pixels, the width of each line.

❖ **Default** selects the current options as the default.

OCR

The OCR tab, which is shown in Figure 10.8, controls the parameters for the OCR tracing method.

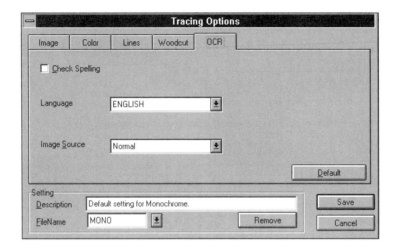

FIGURE 10.8 The OCR tab

❖ **Check Spelling** checks the spelling of the traced text.

Incorrectly spelled words will be omitted, not corrected.

❖ **Image Source** selects the closest origin of the document.
  – Normal.
  – From Dot Matrix.
  – Fax Fine (100 * 200 dpi).
❖ **Default** selects the current options as the default.

Batch Output

You have the option of tracing multiple images in batches. The Batch Files roll-up menu, which is shown in Figure 10.9, controls the parameters for batch operations.

FIGURE 10.9 The Batch Files roll-up menu

Click on the Roll-Up Menu icon in the center of your button bar to display the Batch Files roll-up menu.

SHORTCUT

Tracing Images

Let's start with the basics and trace a simple image using the Outline method.

1. Open a simple bitmapped file by selecting **Open** from the File menu. Select a *.BMP file and click on **OK**.

To select multiple files from the Open Files dialog box, hold down your **Shift** key while clicking on the file names. Select **OK**, and the Batch Files roll-up menu will be displayed.

SHORTCUT

2. Select **Default Settings** from the Settings menu.

3. Select **Outline** from the Trace menu.

Your image appears in the tracing window to the right of the source window.

Tracing Partial Images

To trace partial images, select the Pick tool and use the marquee-select method to select the specific area to be traced. Hold down your **Shift** key to select multiple areas. Then, select the tracing method you want to use.

Partial selection is not available when tracing multiple images.

N O T E

Tracing Images with the Magic Wand Tool

The Magic Wand selects areas of similar color for tracing. This tool is used with the Silhouette tracing method.

CorelTRACE Tips and Tricks

Now that we've talked about the CorelTRACE features, let's review some tips and tricks.

- ❖ Because tracing is slow and uses a great deal of memory, move your images from floppy disk to hard disk before beginning your trace. You should generally reserve about ten times the source file size.

- ❖ Closing any other Windows applications while you trace leaves more memory available, which speeds up tracing time.

- ❖ Keep an eye on your disk space, because traced image files tend to be rather large. To help control your file size:

  - Consider tracing in black-and-white, at a lower resolution.

  - Limit the size of your input images by cropping white space before importing them into CorelTRACE.

❖ Limit the size of your output files by tracing only the portions of the image that you need and by eliminating unnecessary detail (and therefore, extra nodes) from the output image.

Using CorelTRACE can be very much of a trial-and-error process. Until you get the feel for it, you may want to experiment with different settings and options to see what the resulting traced image looks like. Remember, too, that you can import the *.EPS file into CorelDRAW, where you can use all the available tools to add color, modify the outline, and shape the lines and curves.

Summary

This chapter covered how to use CorelTRACE to trace a variety of image types. You can then import the image into CorelDRAW, where you can examine and, if you want, modify the new file. You also saw how using the different options can give you control over the traced images.

Chapter 11

Draw and Shoot: CorelPHOTO-PAINT

CorelPHOTO-PAINT produces paintings and photo-realistic images with its powerful painting tools and retouching capabilities. It also has image and special effects filters to create paintings and images with impact. This chapter covers:

- ❖ The basics
- ❖ Managing CorelPHOTO-PAINT files
- ❖ The display and selection tools
- ❖ The drawing and painting tools
- ❖ The retouching tools
- ❖ Special effects filters

The Basics

When you open CorelPHOTO-PAINT, you see the main screen, which is displayed in Figure 11.1. Many of the operations you perform in CorelPHOTOPAINT are very similar to those in CorelDRAW, including using and moving the toolbox, opening and saving files, and using roll-up menus.

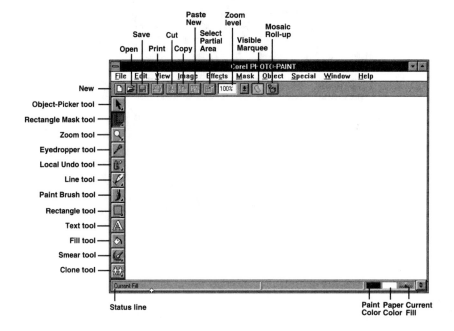

FIGURE 11.1 *The CorelPHOTO-PAINT screen*

The Toolbox

As with the toolbox in CorelDRAW, you can float the PhotoPaint toolbox (using the View menu) and arrange it as ungrouped tools (using the control-bar menu on the floating toolbox).

FIGURE 11.2 The floating toolbox with grouped tools

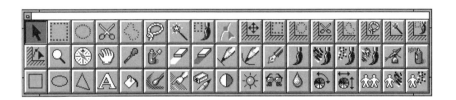

FIGURE 11.3 The ungrouped toolbox

Using the Roll-Up Menus

The CorelPHOTO-PAINT roll-up menus contain most of the controls found in the menu bar and are well suited to painting and retouching because they are similar to working with palettes. There are four main roll-up menus, and all are accessible from the View menu.

The four main roll-up menus are:

❖ **Canvas Roll-Up Menu**, which is shown in Figure 11.4, loads canvas patterns. Once a pattern is applied, it shows through the paint you apply, just as if you were painting on an actual textured surface. To use the roll-up menu, select a canvas pattern using **Load**, click on **Apply**, and then click on **Merge** when you want to save the canvas with the image.

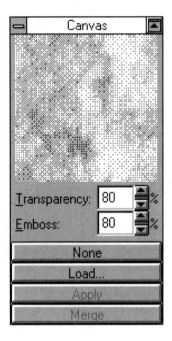

FIGURE 11.4 The Canvas roll-up menu

Press **F3** to display the Canvas roll-up menu.

❖ **Color Roll-Up Menu**, which is shown in Figure 11.5, selects colors for the color table and specifies colors for your painting tools.

Press **F2** to display the Color Selection roll-up menu.

FIGURE 11.5 *The Color Selection roll-up menu*

❖ **Fill Roll-Up Menu**, which is shown in Figure 11.6, has three variations: uniform, import, and texture.

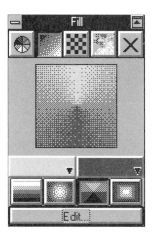

FIGURE 11.6 *The Fill roll-up menus*

Press **F6** to display the Fill Settings roll-up menu.

❖ **Tool Settings Roll-Up Menu**, which is shown in Figure 11.7, controls the shape, width, and effects of the tools. Each tool can be specifically customized so that you can change tools without having to change your settings.

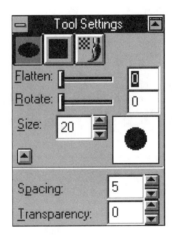

FIGURE 11.7 The Tool Settings roll-up menu

Press **F8** to display the Tool Settings roll-up menu.

Managing CorelPHOTO-PAINT Files

Managing files in CorelPHOTO-PAINT is very similar to managing files in CorelDRAW.

To open an existing file:

1. Select **Open** from the File menu. The Open an Image dialog box is displayed with Options selected in Figure 11.8.

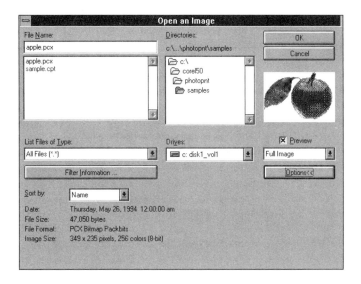

FIGURE 11.8 The Open an Image dialog box with Options selected

Press **Ctrl-O** to display the Open an Image dialog box.

SHORTCUT

2. You can check the Preview box to view a thumbnail of a file.

3. Select the file you want to open from the appropriate directory and click on **OK**.

To open a new drawing file:

1. Select **New** from the File menu. The Create a New Image dialog box is displayed, as shown in Figure 11.9.

SHORTCUT

Press **Ctrl-N** to display the Create a New Picture dialog box.

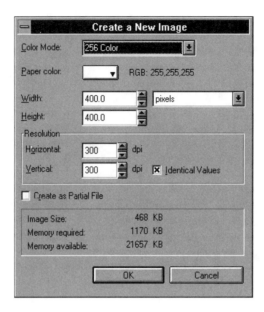

FIGURE 11.9 The Create a New Image dialog box

2. Enter the units of measurement and the measurements for your drawing.

3. Specify a resolution for your file in the Resolution field. A picture's reso-lution can be as high as 1600 dpi.

4. Select the color in the Color Mode field: Black and White, Gray Scale, 16 Color, 256 Color, 24 Bit Color, or 32 Bit CMYK.

N O T E

The dialog box tells you how much memory your settings will require, and how much memory is available on your system.

5. Select **OK**.

The Display and Selection Tools

CorelPHOTO-PAINT has several tools available to let you view and manipulate your work. They let you zoom in and out on an area of your drawing, move your picture, and define areas of your work that you can later cut, copy, or paste.

To illustrate these display and selection tools, let's work with some of the CorelPHOTO-PAINT sample pictures supplied with the software. Let's retrieve one of the pictures now. Click on the File menu and select **Open**. The Load a Open an Image dialog box is displayed.

Make sure your **File Type** is set to ***.PCX**, and that you are in the **COREL\PHOTOPNT\SAMPLES** directory. From the list displayed, highlight **APPLE.PCX**. Double-click on the name (or click once and then click on **OK**), and the picture is displayed on the CorelPHOTO-PAINT screen, as shown in Figure 11.10.

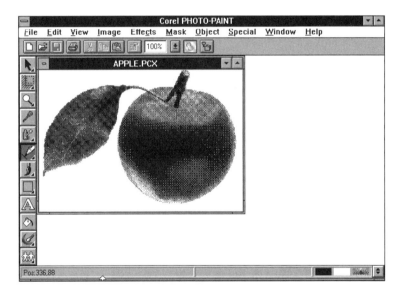

FIGURE 11.10 The apple picture

Open a duplicate of your apple drawing to protect the original. Select **Duplicate** from the Window menu. A duplicate file is created and tagged as **APPLE.PCX:2**.

N O T E

The Display Tools

The Display tools alter the way your picture is displayed on the screen. They include the Zoom, Locator, and Hand tools, which are shown in Figure 11.11.

FIGURE 11.11 The Zoom, Locator, and Hand tools, respectively

The Zoom Tool

To get a close-up of a particular area of your drawing so that you can work with it more accurately, select the Zoom tool. When the magnification cursor appears, move it over the area you want to zoom in on and press the left mouse button. Try moving the cursor over a portion of the apple and zooming in.

Every time you click the left mouse button, the magnification increases. To zoom out again, click on the right mouse button.

You can also use the zoom commands on the View menu to give you more control over the zoom factors.

The Locator Tool

The Locator tool, which looks like a compass, helps you to find a specific location on duplicates of a picture. Click on the Locator tool; then click on the area of the picture you want to see. CorelPHOTO-PAINT displays the area, centered around the area that you clicked, in all copies of the picture.

The Hand Tool

Just as when you're drawing manually (remember that?), you may want to move your "paper" around to get a better view of what you're working on. To do so, click on the Hand tool. Then, press the left mouse button and drag the portion of the picture into view.

The Selection Tools

Use the selection tools to define an area of your picture. The selection tools are shown in Figure 11.12.

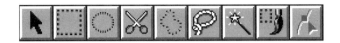

FIGURE 11.12 *The Object Picker, Rectangle Object, Circle Object,
Polygon Object, Freehand Object, Lasso Object, Magic Wand Object,
Object Brush, and Object Node Edit tools, respectively*

The following are some operations that work with all the selection tools:

❖ Hold down the **Shift** key to resize your selection proportionally.

❖ Drag from within the selected portion to move it to another area.

❖ Drag with the left mouse button to make the color opaque.

❖ Drag with the right mouse button to make the color transparent.

❖ Hold the **Shift** key to leave a single copy.

❖ Hold the **Ctrl** key to leave a trail of copies.

Let's look at some of the individual selection tools.

❖ The **Object Picker tool** selects objects.

❖ The **Rectangle Object tool** selects rectangular areas of an image. Click and drag across the area you want to select. After you release the mouse button, you can click on the selected area and manipulate it. To enclose a square area, hold down the **Control** key while you drag the mouse.

❖ The **Circle Object tool** selects circular areas of an image.

❖ The **Polygon Object tool** defines a portion of your drawing in a polygon shape.

1. Click on the Polygon Selection tool (oddly enough, it looks like a scissors) from the toolbox.

2. Point to one corner of the area that you want to select and press the left mouse button.

3. Move the mouse to the end of the first side of the polygon and click again.

4. Continue until you have defined all the sides of the polygon. (Be certain to double-click on your last point, or your polygon selection will go on indefinitely.)

You can also define the area by dragging the mouse. If you want to constrain (restrict) the size of the angle to 45°, hold down the **Control** key while you drag over the area.

❖ The **Freehand Object tool** selects irregular areas of an image. Use it with your left mouse button to select an area and work with only the selected area. Use it with your right mouse button to select an area without selecting the background.

❖ The **Lasso Object** defines any irregular portion of a drawing you want to manipulate.

1. Click on the Lasso tool.

2. Click the left mouse button and drag the mouse over the area you want to "rope in." When the area is enclosed, release the mouse button.

3. Once you've lassoed the area, you can drag it to another portion of your drawing.

❖ The **Magic Wand Object tool** selects areas of similar color. Use the **Color Tolerance** option on the Special menu to adjust the tolerance of this tool. Use this tool to select in a drawing all areas of color with the same hue. This feature is useful for fine-tuning your colors. Let's select the reddest area of the apple.

1. Select the Magic Wand Selection tool.

2. Click on the reddest area of the apple. If you have selected a complex area, this may take a few seconds. Your progress is charted on the lower-left portion of your screen.

3. The selected area is displayed in an active marquee.

❖ The **Object Brush tool** selects the shape of a brush. Select the shape; then choose **Create Brush** from the Special menu.

❖ The **Object Node Edit tool** edits an object using its nodes.

Now that you have the area defined, you can use some of the options from the Edit menu.

Using the Edit Menu with the Selection Tools

When you cut a portion from your drawing, it is placed into the Windows clipboard. The contents of the clipboard can be used in other Corel applications, as well as any other Windows application. Because placing a portion of a picture in the clipboard occupies additional memory, select **Delete** from the Edit menu if you do not want to use that segment later.

The **Copy** option from the Edit menu works almost exactly like the **Cut** option, because the defined area is placed on the Windows clipboard. However, the copied portion remains in your drawing.

You can paste whatever is in the Windows clipboard into your drawing at any time. Select **Paste** from the Edit menu, and the area that you saved is pasted into the upper-left corner of your picture.

The Drawing and Painting Tools

CorelPHOTO-PAINT has several drawing and painting tools you can use to create different effects.

Before we can begin, open a drawing area. Select **New** from the File menu and accept the default values from the Create a New Image dialog box.

Let's discuss the Airbrush, the Spray Can, and the Fill tool, which are best used to fill large areas of your picture. These tools, which are shown in Figure 11.13, can be used to create background or shaded effects or to correct color flaws.

FIGURE 11.13 *The Airbrush, Spray Can, and Fill tools, respectively*

The Airbrush Tool

Use the Airbrush tool to do a freehand spray with the primary color. The Airbrush adds shading and depth to your drawing and corrects flaws. To use the Airbrush tool:

1. Click on the Airbrush tool, and it becomes available with whatever settings you last had.

2. Choose a color from the Color Selection roll-up menu.

3. You can also modify the settings for your airbrush. If you double-click on the Airbrush icon when you select it, the Tool Settings roll-up menu is displayed.

Using the settings shown, let's do some airbrushing in our picture and see what kind of effect the airbrush gives. Once the tool is selected, click and drag the mouse over the area that you want to airbrush. A sample of airbrushing is shown in Figure 11.14.

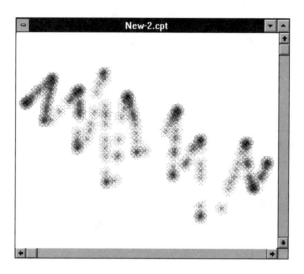

FIGURE 11.14 An example of airbrushing

If you don't like what you've done, there are three ways to get rid of it.

❖   Select **Undo** from the Edit menu, but remember it works only on the last action you performed.

❖   Press **Ctrl-Z** to undo your last command.

❖   Erase it. CorelPHOTO-PAINT also has an Erase tool, but this works a little differently. We discuss the Erase tool later.

The Spray Can

The Spray Can works like a can of spray paint and gives you a splattered type of spray. To use the Spray Can, select the tool; then click and drag it over the area you want to spray. Although the result is somewhat similar to the Airbrush, it gives a much rougher effect, as shown in Figure 11.15.

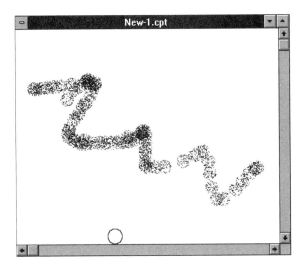

FIGURE 11.15 *An example using the Spray Can*

Just as with the airbrush, you can select another color or change the size and shape of the Spray Can using the Tool Setting roll-up menus.

The Fill Tool

The fill tools are very handy for filling enclosed areas of your picture. Double-click on the Fill tool to open the Fill roll-up menu, which is shown in Figure 11.16.

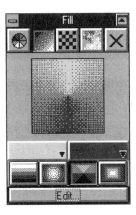

FIGURE 11.16 *The Fill roll-up menu*

An enclosed area can be any part of your picture. For example, if you have a circle or a rectangle, you can fill just that area by placing the small drop inside the shape. On the other hand, if you want to fill your entire picture area, perhaps to create a background effect, you can use the roller. The shape must be fully enclosed or the paint spills out and fills the surrounding area.

To use any fill tool, point to the area you want to fill and click the left mouse button. The drop or arrow at the end of the roller marks the point where the roller begins to fill the area. There are five fill options available from the button bar on the top of the Fill roll-up menu:

❖ **Flood** fills an area with a solid color.

❖ **Gradient** fills an area with a shaded color that shades from the secondary to the background color.

❖ **Tile Pattern** fills the designated area with a repeating pattern, much like wallpaper or floor tile.

❖ **Texture** fills the designated area with a textured background.

❖ **None** leaves an area bare.

All these options work just like their CorelDRAW counterparts. Refer to *Chapter 5* for more details.

You just saw how you can fill rather large areas of your picture with the Airbrush, Spray Can, and Fill tools. Although these options are useful for background work, you can also use them over other objects you've already drawn When you're ready to do some experimenting, try it and look at some of the results you can get.

The Paintbrush Tools

The next four tools—the Paintbrush tool, the Impressionist brush, the Pointillist brush, and the Artist brush—are used to create different painting effects. The painting tools are shown in Figure 11.17.

FIGURE 11.17 *The four paint brush tools—Paintbrush, Impressionist brush, Pointillist brush, and Artist brush, respectively*

❖ The **Paintbrush tool** paints a solid color using the outline color specified in the Color Selection roll-up menu.

❖ The **Impressionist brush tool** paints with multicolored brush strokes.

❖ The **Pointillist brush tool** paints with clusters of dots.

❖ The **Artist brush tool** paints to simulate an oil painting.

Figure 11.18 shows examples of all four brush types.

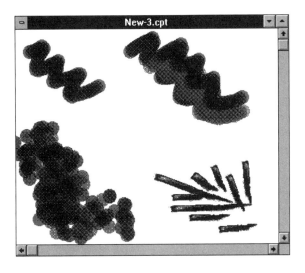

FIGURE 11.18 Examples of all four brush types

To use the painting tools:

1. Double-click on the painting tool you want to use to select it and then select your settings in the Tool Settings roll-up menu.

2. Select the colors you want to use in the Color Selection dialog box.

3. Move the mouse to the place where you want to begin painting; then, click and drag the mouse.

Using Eyedropper and Clone Tools

Use the Eyedropper tool, which is shown in Figure 11.19, to "lift" a color from your picture and replace the fill, outline, or background color. To use the Eyedropper tool:

FIGURE 11.19 *The Eyedropper tool*

1. Click on the Eyedropper tool and point to the color in the picture you want to pick up.

2. Set the color as the primary color by clicking on the left mouse button, the secondary color by clicking on the right mouse button, or the background color by holding the **Ctrl** key while you click the left mouse button.

There are three cloning tools—the Clone tool, the Impressionist Clone tool, and the Pointillist Clone tool—as shown in Figure 11.20.

FIGURE 11.20 *The Clone, Impressionist Clone, and Pointillist Clone tools, respectively*

❖ The **Clone tool** selects an area and duplicates it within a single picture.

❖ The **Impressionist Clone tool** clones colors for the Impressionist brush.

❖ The **Pointillist Clone tool** clones colors for the Pointillist brush.

To use a cloning tool:

1. Double-click on the tool to select it and bring up the appropriate Tool Settings roll-up menu.

2. Click the right mouse button on the source area to define the center point for the source.

3. Point to the area where you want to place the clone and drag using the left mouse button. The cloned image begins to appear as you drag.

4. Release the mouse button when the image you want appears completely.

The Drawing Tools

CorelPHOTO-PAINT has many drawing tools:

- ❖ The Line tool.
- ❖ The Curve tool.
- ❖ The Pen tool.
- ❖ The Rectangle tool.
- ❖ The Ellipse tool.
- ❖ The Polygon tool.
- ❖ The Text tool.

These tools are used for freehand drawing and are displayed in Figure 11.21.

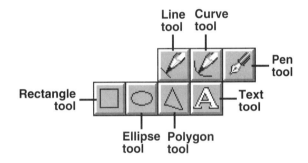

FIGURE 11.21 The drawing tools

Double-click on any drawing tool to select it and display the appropriate Tool Settings roll-up menu. Let's review these tools one by one.

The Line Tool

The Line tool creates straight lines by dragging a line on your picture. The **Shift** key may be used to constrain your line to 45° increments. There are two special effects you can create using the Line tool—joining lines and creating a sunburst effect.

To draw joined lines:

1. Point to where your second line should end and press the right mouse button. A line appears between the end of the first line and where the pointer is positioned.

2. Keeping the right mouse button depressed, position the end of the second line to its exact position and release the mouse.

Lines can be drawn so that their starting point is joined creating a starburst effect. Use the same method as before, but this time also hold the **Ctrl** key joins the line beginnings.

The Curve Tool

Once your tool settings and color selection options are selected, you are ready to draw the curve.

1. Select the point where you want the curve to begin.

2. Drag the mouse to the ending point and release the mouse button. A line appears between the two points, with square handles at the ends and square handles along the line, as shown in Figure 11.22.

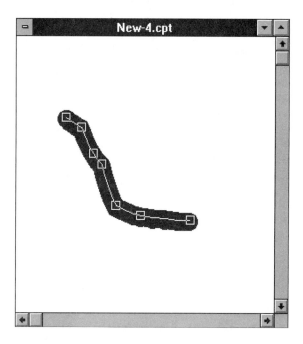

FIGURE 11.22 Beginning a curve

3. To bend the line into the curved shape that you want, drag one of the circular handles in the direction you want the curve to take, as shown in Figure 11.23.

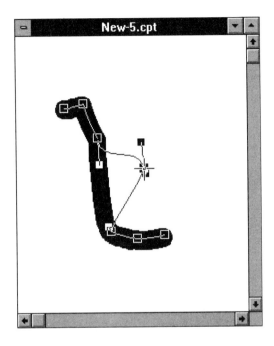

FIGURE 11.23 Repositioning a curve

4. You can further shape the curve by repositioning the end of the curve. To do this, drag on one of the square (end) handles.

5. You can also continue drawing on a curve to create a joined figure. This time you need to use your right mouse button. Point to the area where you want to end the next curve and click the right mouse button. A new curve segment appears, attached to the end of the first one you drew. You can continue adding on to the end of the curve in this way, until you have created a closed shape.

Once your curve is closed, you can use a fill tool to fill the area because it is now enclosed.

N O T E

Another trick you can do with the Curve tool is to join curved rays at a single starting point. For this you will also use the right mouse button.

1. Create a simple curve.

2. Point to the area where you want the next curve to end (don't forget that the starting point is the same as the one you used for the first curve).

3. Hold down the **Ctrl** key and press the right mouse button. A second curve appears.

4. Repeat steps 1–3 as many times as you like, adding a number of curved rays starting at the same point, as shown in Figure 11.24.

FIGURE 11.24 An example of curved rays emanating from a single point

5. You can reshape any of the curves you create by dragging on either the circular handles, to change the curvature, or on the square handles, to reposition the end of the curve.

The Pen Tool

Use the Pen tool to get smooth, even freehand shapes using an outline color. After you've set all your options, press the left mouse button and drag it over the area to draw freehand with the Pen tool.

The Shape Tools (Rectangle, Ellipse, and Polygon)

Use these tools to create shapes bordered by the outline color.

To create a rectangle or ellipse:

1. Select the shape you want from the toolbox.
2. Select the outline color you want for your border from the Color Selection roll-up menu.
3. Set the width of the border in the Tool Settings roll-up menu.
4. Move the mouse to where you want the shape to begin; then click and drag until you have the size you want.

To constrain a box or ellipse to a square or a circle, hold down the **Ctrl** key.

N O T E

When you select the Polygon tool, you can create any multisided shape (with up to 200 sides).

1. Make sure you select the outline color and width.
2. Point to where you want to begin the polygon and click the left mouse button.
3. Point to where you want the first side of the polygon to end and click the left mouse button again.
4. Continue moving the mouse and clicking the left button until the polygon is complete. Be sure to double-click on the ending point.

To constrain the sides of the polygon by a 45° increment, hold down the **Ctrl** key.

N O T E

The Text Tool

Use the Text tool to add text to your picture. Because the text is shown in the fill color, make sure that you have the color you want before you begin. To enter text:

1. Click on the Text tool and select your font, size, and text attributes from the button bar.

2. Click where you want your text to be placed, then enter your text.

Here are some hints for entering text:

❖   You can paste text from the Windows clipboard by pressing **Shift-Ins**.

❖   To break a line in a specific position, press **Ctrl-Enter** using the Enter key on the keypad.

WARNING

Unlike CorelDRAW, you cannot edit the text once it is pasted in the picture.

The Retouching Tools

You may find the retouching tools particularly helpful if you work with photographs or other work you scanned into your system. These tools retouch images by blending, tinting, smudging, or smearing an area. They also brighten or change the contrast in areas of your picture. These tools work with any image format except black-and-white. The retouching tools, shown in Figure 11.25, are:

❖   Local Undo

❖   Erase

❖   Color Replacer

❖   Smear

- ❖ Smudge
- ❖ Sharpen
- ❖ Contrast
- ❖ Brightness
- ❖ Tint
- ❖ Blend
- ❖ Hue
- ❖ Saturation

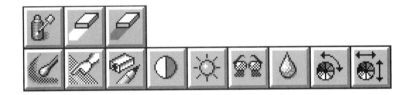

FIGURE 11.25 The Retouching tools

All the freehand retouching tools have a cursor that lets you retouch any area of the picture currently on the screen. As you did with the drawing tools, double-click on the tool you want to use to select it and display the appropriate Tool Settings roll-up menu.

The Eraser Tool

If you decide you don't like any part of what you've drawn, you can use the Eraser to "rub out" a portion of your drawing and change it to the background color. To make it easier to erase, you can adjust the size and shape of your Eraser. Before you use the Eraser, check to see what background color you selected (if by chance it's black and you don't realize it, erasing will have a strange effect).

The Local Undo Tool

Another way of dragging a part of your drawing is by using the Local Undo tool. This tool works like **Undo**, except, that instead of undoing the last operation, you can define an area to be undone. This appears in your toolbox as a bottle of "white out," and this is exactly how it works.

1. Double-click on the Local Undo tool.

2. Adjust the size and width of the tool in the Tool Settings roll-up menu to make sure that it is large (or small) enough to do what you need.

3. Drag the pointer over the areas of the picture that you want to undo.

The Local Undo tool applies only to changes you made since you last selected a tool or command.

N O T E

The Color Replacer Tool

The Color Replacer tool looks exactly like the Eraser, except it has a stroke of color underneath it. When the Color Replacer is selected, it changes the outline color in the area you select to the fill color.

Before you choose the Color Replacer, make sure that you made your paint color the one you wish to change, and your paper color the one you wish the Color Replacer to use for the new color.

N O T E

The Retouching Tools

To illustrate these tools, we will work with the apple picture we used earlier. Copy the image by selecting **1 C:\APPLE.PCX** from the File menu (to protect our original).

❖ The **Smear tool** spreads colors in your picture. You can go over the selected area of your picture several times, until you have the result that you want. Use the Tool Settings roll-up menu to adjust your preferences. Let's smear the apple, as shown in Figure 11.26.

FIGURE 11.26 Smearing a drawing

❖ The **Smudge tool** is another tool for softening the edges in your picture. Just as with the Smear tool, you can drag over an area several times until you get the degree of smudging you need, as shown in Figure 11.27.

FIGURE 11.27 Smudging a drawing

❖ The **Sharpen tool** sharpens areas of your picture that may be too fuzzy. The Sharpen tool lets you go over an area multiple times, until you have the effect you want. This tool can sharpen areas of a picture to separate them from blurred areas.

❖ The **Contrast tool** increases the contrast of any area in your drawing by brightening or darkening any area, as in the left half of the apple in Figure 11.28.

FIGURE 11.28 Using the Contrast tool

❖ The **Brightness tool** changes the intensity of all colors (except black or white). This tool lets you lighten an area to add highlights or darken an area to add shadows, as in the left half of the apple in Figure 11.29.

FIGURE 11.29 Using the Brightness tool

❖ The **Tint tool** alters the colors in an area by applying a type of tinted filter. Before you use the Tint Paintbrush tool on a grayscale picture, convert your picture to 24-bit color. Select **Convert To** from the Image menu; then select **24 Bit Color**. When you select the Tint Paintbrush tool, be sure you have selected the background color that you want to use as your filter. Once you're certain that the brush is the correct size and shape, drag the mouse over the part of the picture you want to change.

❖ The **Blend tool** smoothes and softens transitions by blending two adjacent areas in a 24-bit color or grayscale picture. Like the Contrast and Brighten tools, you can use the Tool Settings roll-up menu to achieve a smoother effect (higher number) or sharper effect (lower number).

Special Effects Filters

Special effects filters, located on the Effects menu, add some interesting results to all or part of an image. Each effect has a preview option, which you should use before applying an effect to ensure that you are getting the desired result. As with other modifications, you can always use the Local Undo or the Erase tool to go back a step.

Depending on the speed of your computer, many of these effects will take some time to apply. The application time increases with the complexity of your image.

N O T E

Some of the special effects filters are

❖ **Pointillism** applies a pointillist effect (dots), as shown in Figure 11.30.

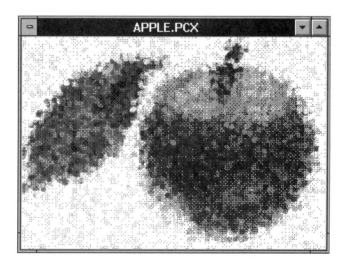

FIGURE 11.30 Applying Pointillism

❖ **Impressionism** adds impressionistic brush strokes, as shown in Figure 11.31.

FIGURE 11.31 Applying Impressionism.

❖ **Edge Detect** (on flyout menu from Fancy option) provides different options for highlighting the edges of an image, as shown in Figure 11.32.

FIGURE 11.32 Applying Edge filters

❖ **Emboss** applies a three-dimensional (raised) effect, as shown in Figure 11.33.

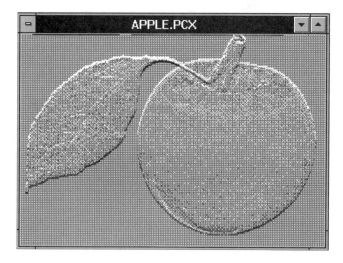

FIGURE 11.33 Embossing an image

❖ **Invert** inverts colors, like a photo negative, as shown in Figure 11.34.

FIGURE 11.34 Inverting an image

❖ **Jaggy Despeckle** scatters the colors in an image.

❖ **Motion Blur** gives the effect of taking a picture of a moving object, as shown in Figure 11.35.

FIGURE 11.35 Applying Motion Blur

❖ **Noise** applies a granular effect to add or remove texture in an image, as shown in Figure 11.36.

FIGURE 11.36 Adding noise to an image

❖ **Posterize** (on flyout menu from the Special option) removes color gradations to produce more even colors, as shown in Figure 11.37.

FIGURE 11.37 *Posterizing an image*

❖ **Psychedelic** (on flyout menu from the Special option) produces a bright, day-glo colorization, as shown in Figure 11.38.

FIGURE 11.38 *Applying a psychedelic filter*

❖ **Solarize** (on flyout menu from the Special option) is similar to an inversion, but with a much softer effect, as shown in Figure 11.39.

FIGURE 11.39 Solarizing an image

Summary

You now know how to use the CorelPHOTO-PAINT selection, drawing, painting, text, retouching, and filter tools to correct and fine-tune your pictures. These tools allow you to sharpen or smooth areas of your drawing or photo, increase or decrease contrast, apply tint, and use special effects filters.

Chapter 12

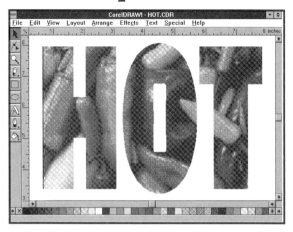

The Ups and Downs: CorelCHART

CorelCHART develops and displays charts that easily and powerfully express complex data. This powerful data manager lets you enter data and calculate results, and it accepts spreadsheet data from Lotus 1-2-3 and Microsoft Excel. It provides line, bar, and pie charts plus true three-dimensional and other specialized chart types.

This chapter discusses:

- ❖ The basics
- ❖ The chart
- ❖ The menus
- ❖ The CorelCHART Data Manager
- ❖ Beginning a chart

The Basics

There are two main elements in CorelCHART.

❖ The Data Manager enters and formats numeric and text data.

❖ Chart View transforms the data into a chart or a graph.

CorelCHART imports spreadsheet data created in other applications, such as Lotus 1-2-3 and Microsoft Excel. You must have Windows 3.1 installed to use True Type fonts and to take advantage of the OLE features of the application.

The CorelCHART screen is basically laid out in the same format as the other Corel applications. Figure 12.1 shows the basic CorelCHART screen. It consists of a title bar; a menu bar, which contains several drop-down menus; a button bar; a tool bar, which is similar to the CorelDRAW toolbox; and the text ribbon, which allows you to control the font size and style of the text you'll be using in your chart. The bottom of your screen displays a color bar, which is convenient for interactively assigning colors to your chart elements.

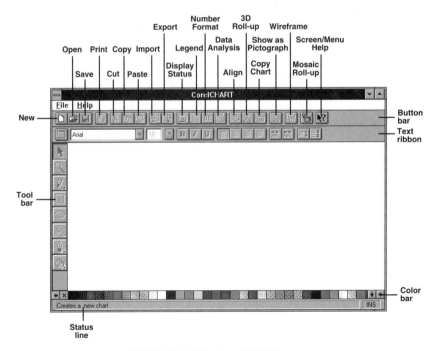

FIGURE 12.1 The CorelCHART screen

The Chart

There are several elements that make up every chart that you work with. Let's look at Figure 12.2 and identify the different parts of a CorelCHART chart. This figure will be useful as we discuss charting and manipulating the data in a chart.

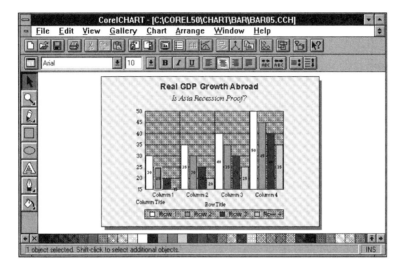

FIGURE 12.2 A CorelCHART chart

Although the chart looks one-dimensional, it consists of two layers. The chart layer contains the titles, footnotes, legends, axis scales, and access titles. The annotation layer is for graphics and other information you add to highlight the features on the chart—in other words, it allows you to further explain your chart.

The Data Manager/Chart View Toggle

The button just above the tool bar toggles between the Data Manager, where you'll be entering or importing data to use in your charts, and the Chart View, where you can see your chart. Only through the Data Manager can you access the numbers and other data that make up your chart. If you've used an electronic spreadsheet before, you will be comfortable working with the CorelCHART Data Manager.

The Context-Sensitive Pop-Up Menu Tool

The context-sensitive pop-up menu tool accesses the menu that controls whichever chart element you are working on. Although you can get to all these options via the menu bar, this tool allows you to see all the items relevant to the particular item you selected in the same place. After selecting the chart element you want to change, click the right mouse button to access the context-sensitive pop-up menu. Figure 12.3 shows the context-sensitive pop-up menus for the Bar Riser.

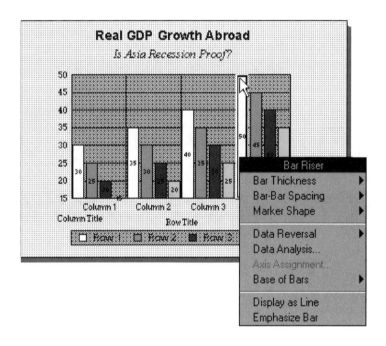

FIGURE 12.3 The context-sensitive pop-up menu for the Bar Riser

The Tool bar

The CorelCHART tool bar, shown floating and ungrouped in Figure 12.4, has the same tools as the CorelDRAW tool bar.

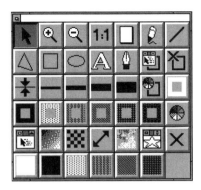

FIGURE 12.4 The CorelCHART tool bar

The Menus

There are many options available on the CorelCHART menu bar. A number of these are available at the click of your mouse on the button bar.

The File Menu

The File menu manages CorelCHART files on disk. You can open a new file by accessing one of the standard chart templates, open an existing file, or write a chart out to disk. Options in the File menu also control the printing of charts.

You can import charts from other applications in the formats shown in Table 12.1.

TABLE 12.1 Importing charts

File Type	File Extension
CorelSheet	*.CDS
CorelSheet 4.0	*.TBL
CSV	*.CSV
Excel 3, 4	*.XLS
Rich Text Format	*.RTF
Text	*.TXT

You can also import graphics images in the formats shown in Table 12.2.

TABLE 12.2 Importing graphics

File Type	File Extension
Adobe Illustrator 1.1, 88, 3.0	*.AI *.EPS
AutoCAD DXF	*.DXF
CompuServe bitmap	*.GIF
Computer graphics metafile	*.CGM
Corel Presentation Exchange	*.CMX
CorelDRAW graphic	*.CDR *.PAT
CorelTRACE	*.EPS
GEM file	*.GEM
HPGL plotter file	*.PLT
IBM PIF	*.PIF
JPEG bitmap	*.JPG *.JFF *.JTF *.CMP
Kodak Photo CD Image	*.PCD
Lotus PICT	*.PIC
Macintosh PICT	*.PCT
Micrografix 2.x, 3.x	*.DRW
Paintbrush	*.PCX
PostScript (Interpreted)	*.EPS *.PS
Scitex CT bitmap	*.SCT *.CT
Targa bitmap	*.TGA *.VDA *.ICB *.VST
TIFF bitmap	*.TIF *.SEP *.CPT
Windows metafile	*.WMF
Windows bitmap	*.BMP *.DIB *.RLE
WordPerfect graphic	*.WPG

If you want to use your charts in other applications, you can export them using the graphics file formats shown in Table 12.3.

TABLE 12.3 Exporting charts

File Type	File Extension
Adobe Illustrator	*.AI, *.EPS
AutoCAD DXF	*.DXF
Comma-separated text	*.CSV
CompuServe bitmap	*.GIF
Computer graphics metafile	*.CGM
CorelSheet	*.CDS
Excel 3.0, 4.0	*.XLS
GEM file	*.GEM
HPGL plotter file	*.PLT
IBM PIF	*.PIF
JPEG bitmap	*.JPG *.JFF *.JTF *.CMP
Macintosh PICT	*.PCT
Matrix/Imapro SCODL	*.SCD
OS/2 bitmap	*.BMP
Paintbrush	*.PCX
Rich Text Format	*.RTF
Scitex CT bitmap	*.SCT *.CT
Tab-separated text	*.TXT
Targa bitmap	*.TGA
TIFF bitmap	*.TIF
Windows bitmap	*.BMP
Windows metafile	*.WMF
WordPerfect graphic	*.WPG

The Edit Menu

Use the Edit menu to undo your last action, duplicate your CorelCHART elements, or cut, copy, or paste to and from the Windows clipboard.

The Gallery Menu

The Gallery menu, shown in Figure 12.5, lets you select a chart type and choose a variation on the chart type. Each chart type has a gray fly-out menu with specific chart type selections as well as a graphic representation of each type.

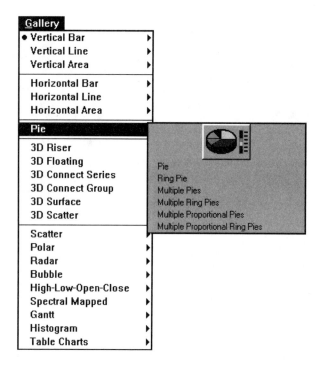

FIGURE 12.5 The Gallery menu

The Chart Menu

The options on the Chart menu manipulate the placement and appearance of items on your chart. The menu selections vary with the type of chart in the active window.

The Arrange Menu

The Arrange menu works like its CorelDRAW counterpart, letting you bring elements in front of or behind other elements.

The Options Menu

The Options menu updates your chart and sets preferences for CorelCHART.

The Window Menu

The Window menu arranges your screen display.

The CorelCHART Data Manager

To create charts using CorelCHART, you need to begin with the data that will make up your chart. To do this, you need to work with the *Data Manager*, the matrix into which you import or enter the basic information that generates in your chart.

Accessing the Data Manager

You can access the Data Manager either by clicking on the Data Manager button directly above the toolbar, or by selecting **Data Manager** from the View menu.

Once you're working in the Data Manager, the Data Manager button transforms into the Chart View tool. In other words, this button lets you switch back and forth between the Data Manager and the Chart View.

The Data Manager Matrix

If you've ever worked with an electronic spreadsheet, the Data Manager screen display, which is shown in Figure 12.6, will look familiar to you. It consists of *columns*, each headed by a letter of the alphabet, and *rows*, each beginning with a number. A *cell* exists at each intersection of a column and a row and is shown as a small box on the screen. Each cell has a location that can be addressed by its row letter and column number. For example, the cell in the upper-left corner of the matrix is cell A1.

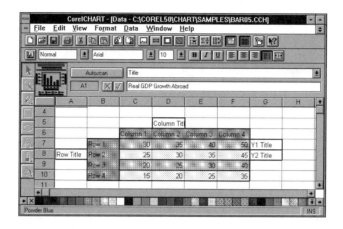

FIGURE 12.6 *The Data Manager screen*

Anatomy of the Matrix

Most of the screen consists of the cells that make up your matrix. However, there are other elements that help you work in the Data Manager. Directly under the menu bar is the button bar, which is shown in Figure 12.7, with lots of handy shortcuts. Under the button bar is the text ribbon, which you can use to specify the typeface, size, style, and justification of the text that you enter into the matrix. Figure 12.8 shows the text ribbon. Directly underneath that, you'll see a bar that displays the tag list. By clicking on the down arrow, you'll see a list of all the types of Data Manager tags.

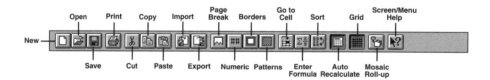

FIGURE 12.7 *The Data Manager button bar*

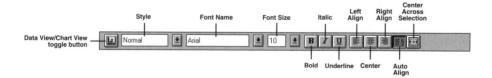

FIGURE 12.8 *The text ribbon*

Working with Cells

To select one particular cell, point to the cell with your mouse and click on it. If you want to select a range of adjoining cells, click on one of the corner cells and drag your mouse diagonally to the opposite corner. To select a group of non-contiguous cells, click on each cell you want while holding down the **Ctrl** key.

Beginning a New Chart

Before we can work with the Data Manager, we must begin building a new chart.

Unlike an electronic spreadsheet, where the information is the basis of the application and the graphic representation follows, CorelCHART is based on the chart—the data in the Data Manager serves to support the representation of that information.

To build a new chart, select **New** from the File menu. The New dialog box, which is shown in Figure 12.9, is displayed. If you are using the CD-ROM version, you will see a shorter list.

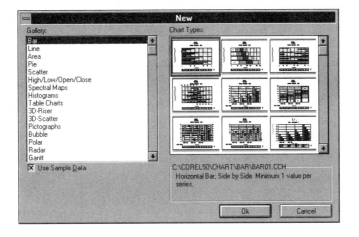

FIGURE 12.9 The New dialog box

If you want to enter your own data and not use the sample data as a template, uncheck the **Use Sample Data** check box. Then select a chart type from the gallery listed in the left side of the dialog box. The gallery previews, graphically displayed on the right side of the dialog box, will help you make your selection.

Click on **OK**, and the Data Manager matrix is displayed on the screen. However, the matrix is blank. You must either import chart data or begin entering data before you can actually show a chart.

Importing Data

Very often you'll want to chart data that you already entered into an electronic spreadsheet, and perhaps have performed a mathematical analysis on. Therefore, you'll need the capacity to import a spreadsheet into CorelCHART.

To import a data file into CorelCHART, select **Import** from the File menu. The Import Data dialog box is displayed.

From the List Files of Type box, select the type of file that you want to import. Locate the correct drive and directory where your data are stored, and from the list of files shown under the File Name box, click on the file name that you want and click on **OK**. Your data are displayed in the Data Manager matrix, as shown in Figure 12.10.

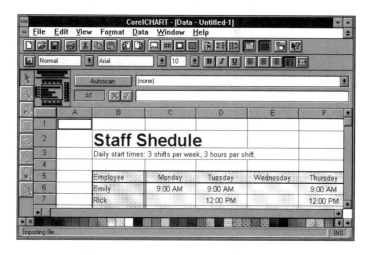

FIGURE 12.10 A Data Manager matrix with imported data

Entering Information in the Matrix

If you have not imported data, you may need to enter all your data from scratch. However, you may also want to enter additional information to add to the data you already imported. Now that you know what rows, columns, and cells are, we can discuss entering information in the data manager.

To select the cell where you want to enter or change data, simply click on the cell with your mouse. Alternately, you can move your cursor into the cell using the arrow keys. Once you enter the data for that cell, you can move on to the next cell you need, either by using the arrow keys or by selecting it with the mouse.

N O T E

The Contents Box just below the Autoscan button displays the cell address on the left side and the data as you type it on the right side.

Tagging Cells

Before you can use any of this information in a chart, you need to tag the cells you want charted. Tagging lets CorelCHART know what each cell (or group of cells) will be used for.

To tag a cell or group of cells:

1. Select the cell or group of cells you want to tag.

2. From the Tag List, click on the type of tag you need. The tag is highlighted.

Using Autoscan to Tag Cells

Tagging cells can get tedious for a complex chart. CorelCHART provides you with an Autoscan feature that automatically tags specific cells for you. Autoscan looks for chart elements in predetermined areas. To tag your cells automatically, place them as shown in Figure 12.11, and then click on the Autoscan button.

	B	C	D	E	F	G
1	Title					
2	Subtitle			Column Title		
3	Footnote			Column Header		
4		Row	Data Range	Data Range	Data Range	
5	Row Title	Headers	Data Range	Data Range	Data Range	Y(Z) Title #1
6			Data Range	Data Range	Data Range	Y(Z) Title #2
7						
8						

FIGURE 12.11 How to arrange your cells for Autoscan

Moving and Reformatting Information

After you import or enter information into the Data Manager matrix, you may find that you want to relocate some of the information. You may also find that you need to resize the cells to accommodate your data, sort the information, or exchange cell data for column data. Here's how it's done.

Moving and Copying Cells

In the Data Manager, you can move or copy any cell or group of cells by using the **Copy**, **Cut**, and **Paste** options from the Edit menu. Select the cell or group of cells that you want to copy or move.

If you want to copy the group of cells (in other words, have the information appear in two locations in the matrix), select **Copy** from the Edit menu. Then, move the cursor to the cell (or the beginning cell) where you wish to place the information and select **Paste** from the Edit menu. The selected cells are copied at the new location.

If, you need to move data (that is, have the data appear at the new location only), choose **Cut** from the Edit menu after you select your cells. Then point to the new location and choose **Paste**. The data are moved to the new location.

When you begin a new chart in the Data Manager, all columns are the same width. However, you may need to change the width of a column, for example, to accommodate longer text elements such as titles, subtitles, and footnotes. To resize a column, move the cursor into the gap between the column headers until it changes from a crosshair to a vertical bar with arrows. Click and drag right or left to move the dividing line between the columns and so change the width of the columns.

Sorting Data

You may want to sort data to rearrange the information in a group of related cells. For example, if you have a group of names, you may want to sort them in alphabetical order. To begin, select the group of cells that you want to sort; then select **Sort** from the Data menu. The Sort dialog box, which is shown in Figure 12.12, is displayed.

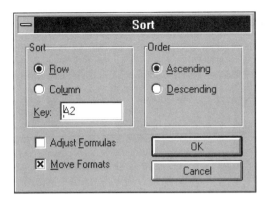

FIGURE *Figure 12.12 The Sort dialog box*

If you want to sort the rows within a column, click on **Rows** and enter the column letter in the Key field. If, however, you want to sort the columns within a row, click on **Columns** and enter the row number in the Key field.

To sort the data in ascending sequence, from lowest to highest, click on **Ascending**. To sort in backward order, click on **Descending**. When you complete all the information in the dialog box, click on **OK**, and the specified data are sorted.

Beginning a Chart

Before we learn how to display data on a chart, let's review some of the fundamentals of beginning a chart. To start a new chart:

1. Select **New** from the File menu.

2. From the Chart Types list, select the chart type that you want. In the first example, we use a bar chart and not sample data, so uncheck the **Use Sample Data** check box. Select **OK** and you'll see the Data Manager screen, but it will be blank because you haven't entered or imported any data.

3. To add some data, select **Import** from the File menu.

4. The chart we'll be working with is the sample file **SCHEDULE.CDS**. Select the file from the file box. Click on **OK**, and the data are displayed in the Data Manager, as shown in Figure 12.13.

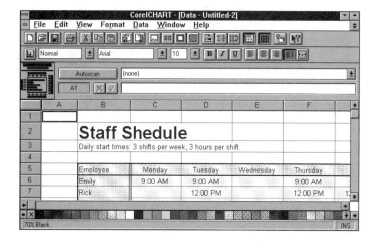

FIGURE 12.13 Imported data in the Data Manager

To see the data charted, click on the Chart View at the top of the tool bar. The bar chart, as shown in Figure 12.14, is displayed on the screen.

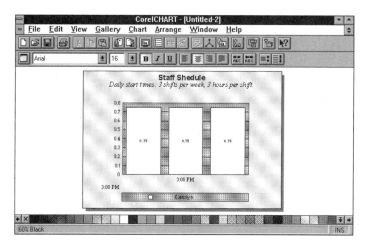

FIGURE 12.14 Imported data charted as a bar chart

If you wish to see both the Data Manager and the chart on the screen at the same time, select **Tile Horizontally** from the Window menu, and the Data Manager and chart are displayed side by side, as shown in Figure 12.15.

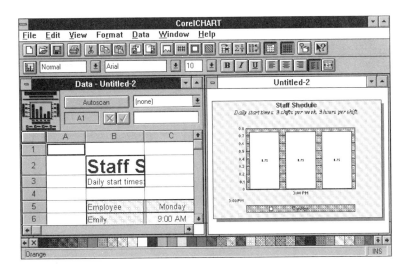

FIGURE 12.15 Chart View and the Data Manager tiled horizontally

Changing a Chart's Appearance

Once the chart is displayed on the screen, you can change any element in the chart by selecting that menu element and accessing the context-sensitive pop-up menu for that element by clicking on the right mouse button after you have selected the element.

Changing the Bar Thickness

Let's start by changing the thickness of the bars on the bar chart. Select the element by clicking on any bar with the left mouse button. Then, click the right mouse button and select the Bar Thickness context-sensitive pop-up menu, as shown in Figure 12.16.

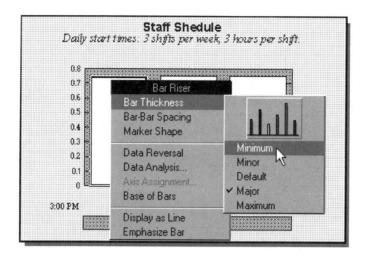

FIGURE 12.16 The Bar Thickness pop-up menu

To see how really easy this is, select a bar, click on the right mouse button, and select **Minimum** from the Bar Thickness fly-out menu. The chart is redrawn, as shown in Figure 12.17.

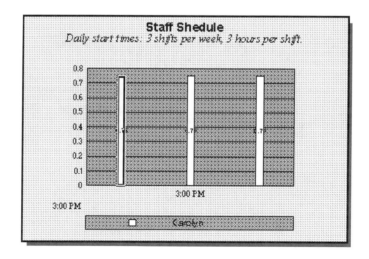

FIGURE 12.17 The bar thickness set to Minimum

Reversing the Data

You may want to see how the data look reversed. To reverse the data, select **Data Reversal** from the Chart menu and, from the pop-up menu shown, select **Reverse Series**.

Scale and Grid

Often, the same data can look quite different, depending on the scale they are displayed in. For example, using a different scale can eliminate more extreme numbers from a chart.

When CorelCHART draws a chart using the automatic scale range, it sets the scale to include the highest and lowest values represented in the data. Changing the scale can both alter a chart's appearance and change how the numbers appear relative to each other.

To change the scale on the Y (vertical) axis, click on any number along the axis and then click the right mouse button. From the pop-up menu shown, select **Scale Range**, and the Scale Range dialog box, which is shown in Figure 12.18, is displayed. Use the Manual Scale From and To value boxes to flatten or lengthen the bars.

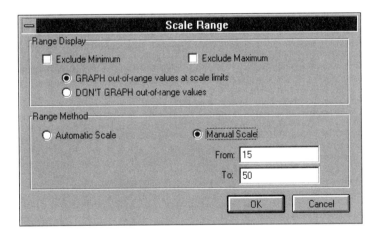

FIGURE 12.18 The Scale Range dialog box

You can make your chart a little easier to read by adding grid marks. Click on any number along the axis and click the right mouse button. From the pop-up menu, select **Grid Lines**, and the Grid Lines dialog box, shown in Figure 12.19, is displayed. From the Major Divisions option on the left side of the dialog box, check **Show Major Grid Lines**; then click on **Normal with Ticks**. At the bottom, click on **Auto** and click on **OK**. The chart reappears with grid lines along the vertical axis.

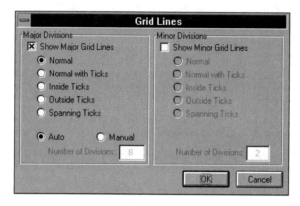

FIGURE 12.19 The Grid Lines dialog box

Choosing Another Chart Type

CorelCHART makes it very easy for you to change chart types on the fly, letting you experiment and see which type of chart best represents the data. To see how these data would look as a three-dimensional riser chart, choose **3D Riser** from the Gallery menu. From the fly-out menu shown, choose **Bars**. The chart reappears, as shown in Figure 12.20.

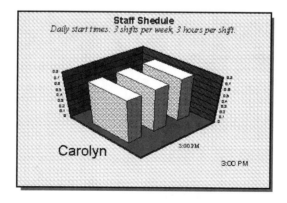

FIGURE 12.20 The 3D riser bar chart

On a 3D riser bar chart, you can also change the viewing angles of the bars in the chart. From the Chart menu, select **Preset Viewing Angles**. From the fly-out menu shown, select **Distorted**. Figure 12.21 shows how your chart looks with the Distorted viewing angle selected.

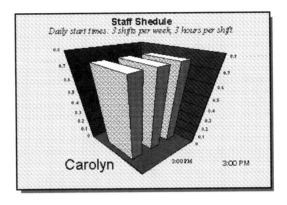

FIGURE 12.21 The 3D riser bar chart with the Distorted viewing angle

The contents of the Chart menu vary with the type of chart with which you are currently working.

In addition to the vertical bar charts that we've worked with, you can also display data horizontally, as shown in Figure 12.22.

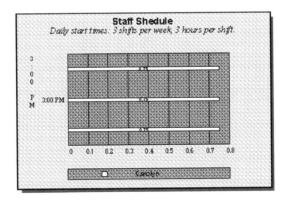

FIGURE 12.22 A horizontal bar chart

Adding Fills

While we're looking at this chart, let's see how we can spruce it up a bit. Adding a texture fill to enhance your chart works the same way that it does in CorelDRAW. Select any object (let's choose the background); then select the Texture Fill button from the Fill tool fly-out menu. The Texture Fill dialog box, shown in Figure 12.23, is displayed. Select the texture you want for the selected element and click on **OK**. The fill is applied to your chart, as shown in Figure 12.24.

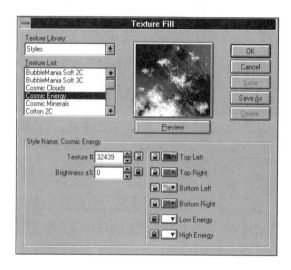

FIGURE 12.23 The Texture Fill dialog box

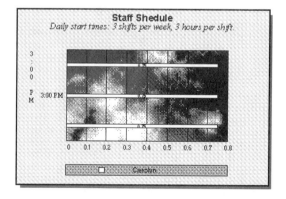

FIGURE 12.24 A texture fill applied to bar a chart

Displaying a Chart on the Screen

While you are working with your chart, it's a good idea to make the view of the chart as large as possible and to display all the chart elements on the screen. However, you may wish to display or hide certain elements to make your chart easier to understand. To help you display or hide elements, select **Display Status** from the Chart menu. The Display Status dialog box, which is shown in Figure 12.25, is displayed.

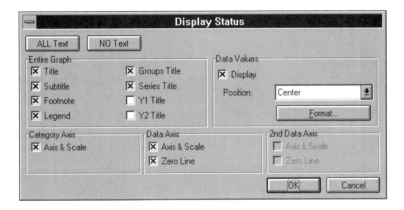

FIGURE 12.25 The Display Status dialog box

Turn on the elements you want to show and turn off the elements you want to hide. Then click on **OK** and look at the revised view of your chart. You can also enlarge the entire view of the chart on the screen by resizing the window.

Using Text and Graphics

You can change the look of your chart by changing the fonts for any text element in your chart. Click on the text you want to change. From the text ribbon at the top of the screen, select the font you want from the list box in the left corner. From the text ribbon, you can amend the style as well as the font by using the style icons. You can also change the point size or justification from the text ribbon.

To further explain the data shown in your chart, add an annotation anywhere on the chart. Select the text tool; then drag a text frame over the area of the chart where you want to place the annotation. Once the frame is placed, type in your text.

Adding a Graphic

You can include a graphic on your chart to give it some pictorial interest. You can use one of the symbols in your True Type font set, or you can import a graphic from CorelDRAW.

Selecting the Best Chart Type

As you can see, CorelCHART offers a variety of chart types. Experiment with any type you like, but certain types of data are best represented by one or more specific types of charts.

Bar Charts

Use *vertical bar charts* to show how data change over time, for example, comparing the information for several years. A variation on the bar chart is the *stacked bar*, which can show how different parts contribute to a whole. For example, if a bar chart showed the performance of a company over several years, a stacked bar chart can show how much profit each division of the company generated in each of the years displayed.

Several variations on the vertical bar chart represent the same information in a different way. You can also enliven a bar chart by creating a pictograph. Select one of the bars; then, from the Chart menu, choose **Show as Pictograph**. Then, from the Fill fly-out menu on the tool bar, select the **Pictograph** (the roll-up menu icon with a star). Import one of the available patterns and apply it to your chart. Figure 12.26 shows a bar chart illustration as a pictograph. Horizontal bar charts are good for representing variations in values within a specific time frame.

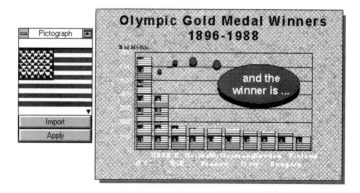

FIGURE 12.26 A bar chart illustrated as a pictograph

Line Charts

Now let's take a look at another of the major chart types, the *line chart*. This type of chart works better if your values represent changes in a small group of values over a long period of time. Figures 12.27, 12.28, and 12.29 show a line chart, a 3D ribbon chart, and a vertical area chart, respectively.

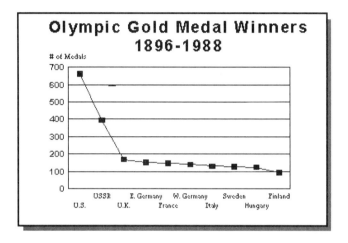

FIGURE 12.27 A line chart

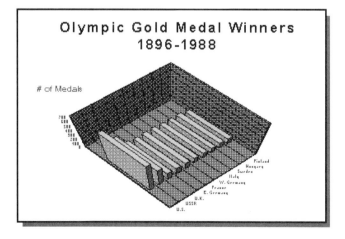

FIGURE 12.28 A 3D ribbon chart

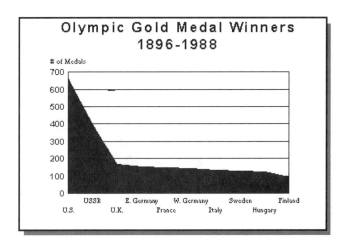

FIGURE 12.29 A vertical area chart

Pie Charts

Pie charts are most effective if you want to show how different parts contribute to a whole (in other words, to show percentages). Figure 12.30 shows a ring pie chart. To represent the same type of data over a period of time, use multiple pie charts, as shown in Figure 12.31

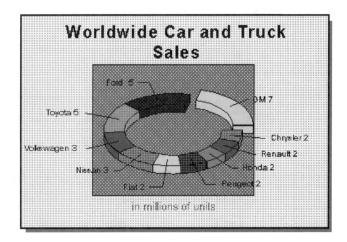

FIGURE 12.30 A ring pie chart

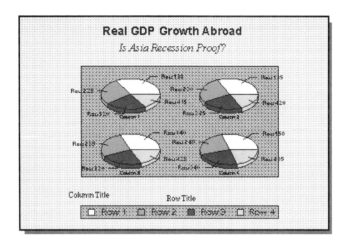

FIGURE 12.31 Multiple pie charts

The best way to decide which type of chart to use is to begin with some of these basic guidelines and then experiment. Because CorelCHART makes it so easy to redraw a chart with any type from its gallery, you can preview what each selection will look like and make changes at any time.

Summary

In this chapter, you learned how to use the basics of CorelCHART to chart any information and visually present it in the best way possible.

Chapter 13

Creating a CorelSHOW Presentation

CorelSHOW lets you put together objects from a variety of applications and create a presentation consisting of multiple pages or slides.

This chapter covers:

- ❖ Getting started
- ❖ The presentation screen
- ❖ Creating a slide show

Input for CorelSHOW can come from CorelDRAW, CorelCHART, or any other application that supports object linking and embedding. CorelSHOW does not actually create objects but presents existing objects for output in the form of animated screen shows, slides, overheads, or series of panels that you can print later. If you're creating an on-screen presentation, you can be a real filmmaker, deciding how long each image remains on the screen and using transition effects to make a more professional move from one view to the next.

For the sake of this discussion, we will call each page or view of a presentation a *slide*.

N O T E

CorelSHOW is an *OLE assembler program*, which means that it can link or embed an object from CorelDRAW, CorelCHART, or any other server application. When you embed an object, you actually insert information from the source file (in this instance, the CorelDRAW or other file) into the destination document in another application (such as CorelSHOW). If you link the object, you do not insert the file information, but only the link to the object's location. When linked or embedded objects are edited, their source application is opened to provided the necessary tools. To use OLE to link and embed objects, you must be running under Windows 3.1.

Getting Started

First let's define a few terms. A *background* is exactly what it implies—it is the backdrop against which a slide is viewed. If you've ever been to a photographer's studio, think of it as the drape that is placed behind you to give a particular effect to your portrait.

There are several ways of viewing or editing a presentation:

- ❖ **Slide View** views and edits individual slides. CorelSHOW allows multiple document viewing, letting you open several files at one time and move or copy information from one file to another.
- ❖ **Background View** edits the background of each slide.
- ❖ **Speaker Notes View** displays the speaker notes with a thumbnail of the current slide.
- ❖ **Slide Sorter View** views the entire presentation.

The Presentation Screen

To open CorelSHOW, double-click on its icon in the Corel group, then click on **New Presentation** button. The CorelSHOW screen has several elements, as shown in Figure 13.1.

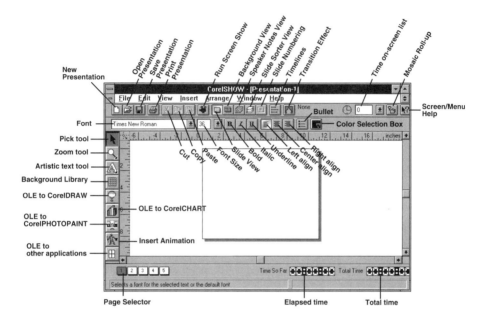

FIGURE 13.1 The CorelSHOW screen

The CorelSHOW Menu

The top line of the screen includes the name of the application, CorelSHOW. The next line is the menu bar, which lists the following items:

❖ **File** opens, saves, closes, prints files, and runs a screen show.

❖ **Edit** cuts, copies, and pastes operations, or undoes a previous command.

❖ **View** places rulers and guidelines to help you arrange the presentation.

❖ **Insert** inserts, embeds, or links an object, animations, sounds, and files into a slide show.

❖ **Arrange** organizes objects on top of each other.

❖ **Window** manages the presentation windows on the screen.

❖ **Help** accesses CorelSHOW interactive help.

As with other Corel applications, you may use the button bar below the menu bar to access many features quickly.

The Toolbox

The toolbox along the left edge of the screen shows the following tools:

❖ The **Pick tool** selects, moves, or resizes objects.

❖ The **Zoom tool** changes the viewing magnification on your screen.

❖ The **Artistic Text tool** adds text to a slide.

❖ The **Background Library tool** selects backgrounds for a slide show.

❖ The **OLE to CorelDRAW tool** provides a gateway to CorelDRAW files.

❖ The **OLE to CorelCHART tool** provides a gateway to CorelCHART files.

❖ The **OLE to CorelPHOTO-PAINT tool** provides a gateway to CorelPHOTO-PAINT files.

❖ The **Insert Animation tool** places an animation on the current slide.

❖ The **OLE to Other Applications tool** accesses any other applications that support OLE.

To make your toolbox a floating palette, select **Floating Toolbox** from the Toolbox fly-out menu under the View menu and move your toolbox by clicking on its title bar and dragging it to the new location.

Viewing Mode Buttons

On the button bar are four buttons that represent the three viewing modes:

❖ **Slide View** lets you view and edit the individual slides on which you are working while you assemble the slides in your show. When you're working in Slide View, you can use the tools in the toolbox to access objects from other applications.

❖ **Background View** views and edits the background that you will use for each slide in the show. To let you work directly on the background, the slide show disappears. While you are working in Background View, you can use the tools in the toolbox to access objects from other applications.

❖ **Speaker Notes View** views and edits the speaker notes for a current slide. A speaker notes page exists for every slide in a presentation and is saved with the presentation file. These pages can even be printed.

❖ **Slide Sorter View** gives you a miniaturized view of each slide in the show. If all of your slides do not fit on the screen, use the vertical scroll bars to page through the slides. Use the Slide Sorter View button to arrange the slides in your show by dragging the slides around the window to a new location, or you can access the **Cut**, **Copy**, and **Paste** options from the Edit menu. If you move one slide while you're working in this mode, all others automatically move to accommodate the change.

When you choose the Slide Sorter View button, a Numbering tool becomes active to the right of the button. Use the Numbering tool to number the slides in the show. By clicking in succession on each slide in the show, you can rearrange the slides without physically moving them around. When you've numbered all of the slides, click again on the Numbering tool, and the slides are rearranged on the screen.

Transition Effects

Click on the Slide Transition button to see the Transition Effects dialog box, which is shown in Figure 13.2.

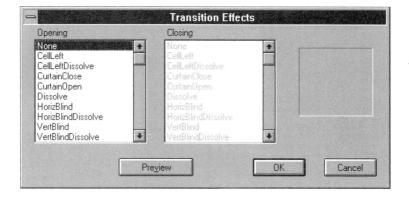

FIGURE 13.2 The Transition Effects dialog box

Use this dialog box to specify transitions between each slide. These are the transition effects you can choose:

- ❖ CellLeft
- ❖ CellLeftDissolve
- ❖ CurtainClose
- ❖ CurtainOpen
- ❖ Dissolve
- ❖ HorizBlind
- ❖ HorizBlindDissolve
- ❖ VertBlind
- ❖ VertBlindDissolve
- ❖ WipeDown
- ❖ WipeLeft
- ❖ WipeRight
- ❖ WipeUp
- ❖ ZoomIn
- ❖ ZoomInSlow
- ❖ ZoomInFast
- ❖ ZoomInDissolve
- ❖ ZoomOut
- ❖ ZoomOutSlow
- ❖ ZoomOutFast
- ❖ ZoomOutDissolve

Time On-Screen

Use the **Time on-screen** list field to specify the amount of time the selected slide remains on the screen.

Timelines

Use the Timelines button to view and coordinate the timing of all slides and objects in your screen shows. Click once on the Timelines button to display the Timelines for Presentation dialog box, which is shown in Figure 13.3.

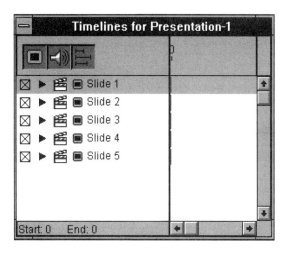

FIGURE 13.3 The Timelines for Presentation dialog box

Page Icons

On the lower-left of the screen (above the status line) are the icons of all the slides in the current presentation. The slide on which you are currently working is shown in gray. Click once on a page icon to move directly to the slide on which you want to work.

Show Clocks

In the lower-right corner of the screen, you'll see *Show Clocks*, which displays the total running time of the slide show and the time that has elapsed so far.

Creating a Slide Show

To illustrate how to create a slide show presentation, use the sample show included with CorelSHOW:

1. Select **New** from File menu. Make sure you have five slides specified in the **Start with** field.

2. Click on **Page Setup**.

3. From the Page Setup dialog box, choose **Screen** and then click on **OK**.

4. Click on **OK** to accept your settings and return to the CorelSHOW screen.

Choosing the Background

Let's begin assembling the slide show by choosing the background:

1. Click on the Background View button on the toolbox.

2. Select **C:\corel50\show\backgrds\sample.shb** in the Open File dialog box, which is shown in Figure 13.4. Make sure the **List Files of Type** field is set to ***.SHB**.

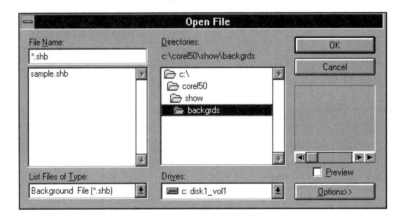

FIGURE 13.4 The Open File dialog box

3. Click on **OK**. Figure 13.5 graphically shows the backgrounds that are available in the library.

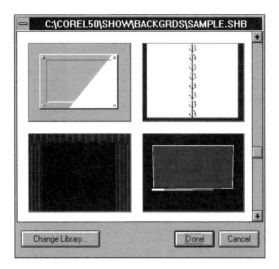

FIGURE 13.5 The available backgrounds

Selecting the Slides

The slides we want to use in our presentation are in CorelDRAW and CorelCHART. We will also use an animation file to add excitement to our presentation.

Linking to OLE Files

Use the OLE buttons on the bottom of the toolbar to add files from CorelDRAW, CorelCHART, CorelPHOTO-PAINT, CorelMOVE or any other OLE-supporting application.

If you want to edit the object, double-click on it. This returns you to your source application, where you can make your changes. When you're done, select **Copy** from the Edit menu, close the application, and return to CorelSHOW.

The Slide Sorter

If you'd like to rearrange the slides, click on the Slide Sorter button. Click on the slide you want to move and drag it to a new location. Release the mouse button, and the slides are now rearranged.

Saving a Slide Show

To save a slide show, select **Save As** from the File menu. In the Save Presentation As dialog box, which is shown in Figure 13.6, name the new file. You can also add keywords or notes to the file to jog your memory when you retrieve it later.

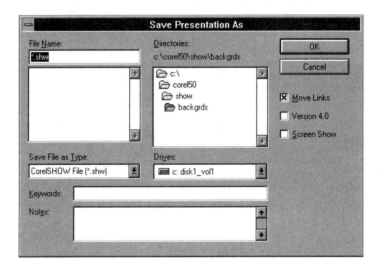

FIGURE 13.6 The Save Presentation As dialog box

Viewing a Slide Show

To see how your slide show turned out, select the Run Screen Show button. Because you've already saved it, feel free to make any changes you'd like to the color, transitional effects, or even the content of the slides themselves. Because these are OLE objects, you can always go back to the source application and edit them in whatever way you want.

Summary

In this chapter you learned how to use the CorelSHOW application to assemble objects from a variety of applications and arrange them into a slide show (or screen presentation). You've also seen how to use CorelSHOW to assemble various elements in a slide show.

Chapter 14

Lights, Camera, Action: CorelMOVE

CorelMOVE is an animation program that simulates the traditional frame-by-frame method of animation. You create a series of drawings linked together to give an illusion of movement. However, rather than having to draw each cel individually, as in the traditional method, CorelMOVE can create intermediary cels in an actor's movement. It also allows you to add sound effects and to layer multiple animated images and sounds. This chapter covers:

- ❖ The menus
- ❖ The toolbox
- ❖ The control panel
- ❖ The roll-up menus
- ❖ Creating an animation
- ❖ Creating objects

To open CorelMOVE, double-click on its icon in the Corel group. The CorelMOVE screen is displayed. This screen is initially blank, except for the File menu, until you open or create an animation. Select **New** from the File menu. In the Select Name For New File dialog box, which is shown in Figure 14.1, type in a name for your new animation and click on **OK**. The complete screen is displayed in Figure 14.2.

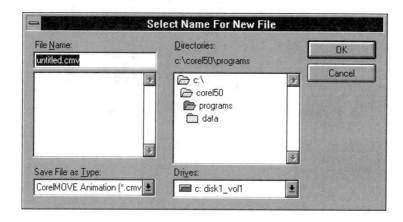

FIGURE 14.1 The Select Name For New File dialog box

FIGURE 14.2 The CorelMOVE screen

The Menus

The top line of the screen includes the name of the application and current file, followed by the menu bar. The menu bar contains the following items:

❖ **File** opens new and existing animations, saves animations, and provides importing and exporting functions.

❖ **Edit** offers cut-and-paste options, as well as duplication, cloning, and object editing.

❖ **View** lets you view the different frames of your animation, as well as play and stop your animation.

❖ **Arrange** allows you to change the placement of objects.

❖ **Help** provides on-screen help.

In the center of the screen is the animation window in which you create and edit your animations.

The Toolbox

The toolbox, on the left of the screen, contains the following items:

❖ The **Pick tool** selects and scales objects.

❖ The **Path tool** creates paths on which objects are placed.

❖ The **Actor tool** adds and creates new actors.

❖ The **Prop tool** adds and creates new props.

❖ The **Sound tool** adds new sounds.

❖ The **Cue tool** adds and creates cues.

The Control Panel

The control panel is located on the bottom of your screen. It contains the following items:

❖ The **Show Timelines button** accesses the Timelines roll-up menu.

❖ The **Library button** accesses the Library roll-up menu.

- ❖ The **Cel Sequencer** accesses the Cel Sequencer roll-up menu.
- ❖ The **Sound button** turns the sound on and off.
- ❖ The **Loop button** places the animation in a continuous play mode.
- ❖ The **playback controls** work just like your VCR to control playback, reverse, fast forward, and stopping actions.
- ❖ The **frame counter** lets you know how many frames you have. The current frame number is on the left, and the total number of frames is on the right.
- ❖ The **status line** provides information about the selected object.

You can toggle the control panel on or off from the View menu.

The Roll-Up Menus

There are three roll-up menus in CorelMOVE: Timelines, Cel Sequencer, and Library. All three are accessible from the View menu or the control panel on the bottom of your screen.

Timelines

The Timelines roll-up menu, which is displayed in Figure 14.3, lets you view and edit the elements of an animation.

FIGURE 14.3 The Timelines roll-up menu

The object icons at the top of the menu represent the objects in your animation—actors, props, sounds, and cues. The object list displays the name and type of each object. Double-click on an object to get information about it.

The slider indicates the amount of the animation that is visible in the window.

The timelines window, which looks like a graph, displays the amount of time each object spends in the animation.

Cel Sequencer

The Cel Sequencer roll-up menu, which is shown in Figure 14.4, combines actor cels with animation frames. An actor must be selected for options to be available.

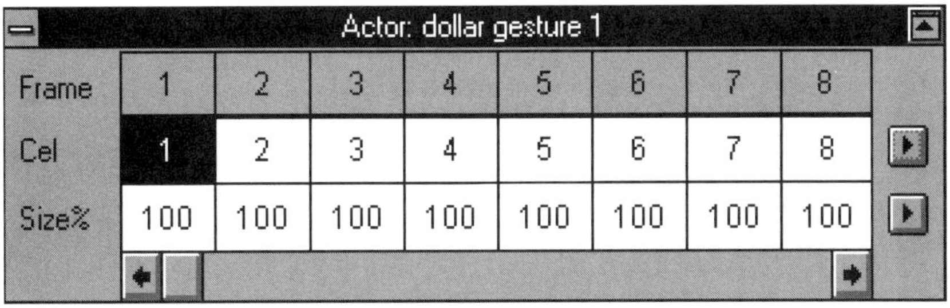

Actor: dollar gesture 1								
Frame	1	2	3	4	5	6	7	8
Cel	1	2	3	4	5	6	7	8
Size%	100	100	100	100	100	100	100	100

FIGURE 14.4 The Cel Sequencer roll-up menu

When you create an actor, you specify the number of cels to which the actor is assigned to create an illusion of movement. The Cel Sequencer roll-up menu lets you reassign the sequence of an actor's cels.

Library

The Library roll-up menu creates and stores libraries of animation objects. The two modes, visual and text, are shown in Figure 14.5. Turn the visual mode on and off using the last option on the fly-out menu.

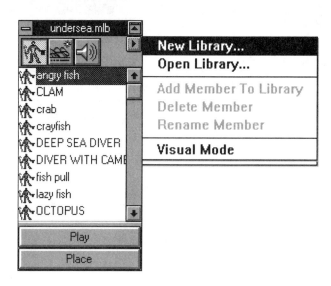

FIGURE 14.5 The visual and text Library roll-up menu with fly-out menus

You can also use the fly-out menu to create new libraries, open existing libraries, add objects to libraries, delete objects from libraries, and rename objects within libraries.

Creating an Animation

Let's use the sample library to create a simple animation:

1. Select **New** from the File menu. Name your animation in the Select Name For New File dialog box and click on **OK**.

2. Choose **Animation Info** from the Edit menu. In the Animation Information dialog box, which is shown in Figure 14.6, enter the size of your animation screen, the number of frames you want, the speed per second of your frames, and the grid spacing. Accept the default settings and click on **OK**.

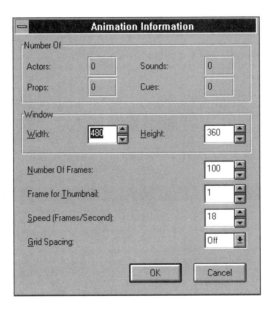

FIGURE 14.6 The Animation Information dialog box

3. Click on the Library icon on the control panel to display the Library roll-up menu. The button bar on the top of the menu lets you select actors, props, and sounds.

4. Click on the Prop button and select the **Prehistoric** prop. Click on **Place** and then select the placed prop using your Pick tool. Move the anchor to the lower-right corner of your screen, as shown in Figure 14.7.

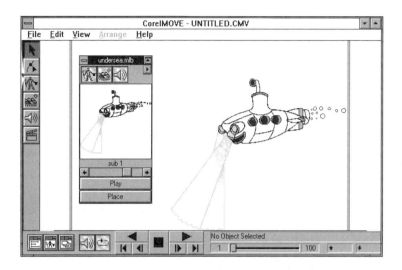

FIGURE 14.7 A prop placed in an animation

5. Click on the Actor button and select the **Baby Dino**. Click on **Play** and preview the movement of the actor. Click on **Stop Playing** and then click on **Place** to use this actor. Move it to the lower-left corner of your screen, as shown in Figure 14.8.

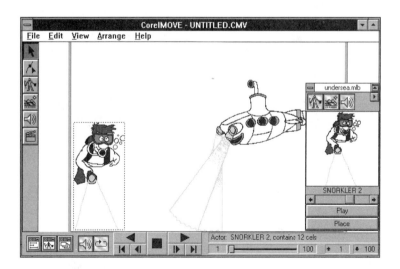

FIGURE 14.8 An actor added to an animation

6. Add the **Little Dino Fast** Run and place it on the top of your screen.

7. Click on the Play button on the control panel to view your animation, as shown in one frame in Figure 14.9.

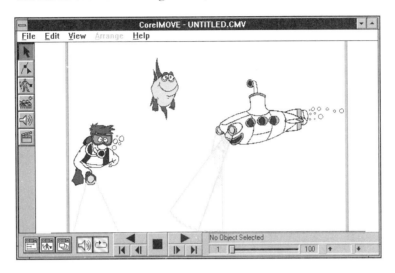

FIGURE 14.9 One frame of an animation

8. Save your animation using the **Save** option from the File menu.

Creating Objects

You can use the Actor and Prop tools on the toolbox to create your own actors and props in CorelMOVE or to add actors and props from other Corel modules.

Creating Objects in Other Programs

To import objects from other Corel modules, click on the name of the module in the New dialog box that is displayed when you select a tool. Select the object type, click on **Create from File**, and click on **OK**.

Creating Objects in CorelMOVE

To create new objects in CorelMOVE, click on **CorelMOVE 5.0** in the New dialog box, select **Create New**, and click on **OK**. Use the drawing tools, which are shown in Figure 14.10, as you would in CorelPHOTO-PAINT to draw an object.

FIGURE 14.10 The new drawing tools and window

❖ The **Marquee tool** selects a rectangular area when you click and drag it.

❖ The **Lasso tool** selects a specific area of an object.

❖ The **Pencil tool** draws freehand lines.

❖ The **Brush tool,** which has a fly-out menu with different brush shapes, paints with the currently selected pattern or color.

❖ The **Paint Bucket (fill) tool** fills an enclosed area using the currently selected color and pattern.

❖ The **Spraycan tool** produces an airbrush effect using the currently selected color and pattern.

❖ The **Text tool** inserts text into an object.

❖ The **Eraser tool** removes a portion of an image.

❖ The **Color Pick-up (eyedropper) tool** selects a color from one part of an image to be used in another part of an image.

❖ The **Line tool** draws straight lines.

- ❖ The **Rectangle tool** draws rectangles and squares.

- ❖ The **Rounded Corner Rectangle tool** draws rectangles and squares with rounded corners.

- ❖ The **Ellipse tool** draws ellipses and circles.

- ❖ The **Curve tool** draws free-form curved shapes.

- ❖ The **Polygon tool** draws multisided forms. Be certain to double-click on the last segment of your polygon, or it will go on indefinitely.

- ❖ The **foreground and background selectors** specify the colors used in the image.

- ❖ The **line width selector** specifies the width of the lines in your drawing tools.

- ❖ The **pattern selector** specifies a pattern to be applied to your objects.

Use the choices on the Options menu to specify special effects on a cel-by-cel basis.

Select **Apply Changes** from the File menu to accept your new object and place it on the animation screen. Once you create an object, you can add it to a library to use later.

Animating an Actor

Props are *static*—hey have no movement. Actors, however, are basically props that have had movement—animation—applied to them.

N O T E

Only actors can be animated. If you create or import a prop, you cannot animate it. You must recreate it as an actor or import it as an actor.

To animate an actor, you must place it on a path. To do this:

1. Place an object on your screen.

2. Select it using the Pick tool.

3. Select the Path tool and begin clicking the points of your path, as shown in Figure 14.11. Your actor will appear to move as it follows these points.

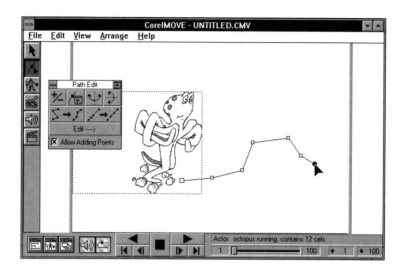

FIGURE 14.11 Adding a path

4. You can add special effects to all or specific points of your path by using the options in the Cel Sequencer roll-up menu or by using the Sound or Rotation buttons on the control panel.

You must have a sound board installed to use or play back sound effects.

N O T E

5. View the animation of your object by clicking on the Play button on your control panel.

Creating Multiple Cel Actors

There are two types of animation in CorelMOVE. We have already covered the first kind, movement along a path. The second type is the movement of an actor itself, which is independent of its path. The number of cels an actor has controls its speed and the illusion of its movement.

To insert cels in an actor, double-click on an actor. From the Actor Information dialog box, select **Edit Actor**, and the Actor editor window is displayed.

Select **Insert Cels** from the Edit menu, type in the number of cels and cel specifications and then select **OK**.

To remove a cel, select **Delete Cels** from the Edit menu. In the Delete Cels dialog box, specify the number of cels to be deleted and then click on **OK**.

To illustrate the difference between cel animation and path animation, open the Library roll-up menu and scroll until you find the running octopus, which is shown in Figure 14.12.

FIGURE 14.12 The running octopus

Click on **Play**, and in the view window you will see the cel animation of the octopus. This action is built into the actor itself. Click on **Place** to add it to your screen.

Click on the Play button on the control panel, and you will see the same animation you saw in the view window of the library. Notice, however, that the octopus runs in place—its legs move but the octopus itself doesn't go anywhere. Let's change that.

1.   Select the Path tool and click on the octopus.

2.   Create a path for the octopus to follow, going from left to right, as shown in Figure 14.13.

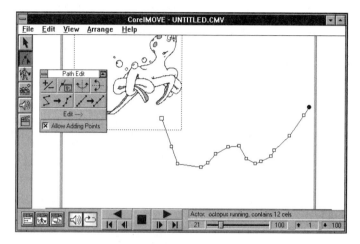

FIGURE 14.13 *Adding a path to the octopus*

3.   Click on the Play button on the control panel to view the combined animation of the cel and the path, as shown in Figure 14.14.

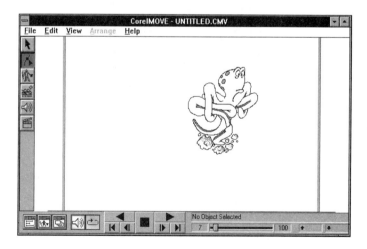

FIGURE 14.14 *The completed cel and path animation*

Adding Sound

To create a new sound effect:

1. Select the Sound tool from the toolbox. The New Wave dialog box is displayed.

2. Enter the name of your sound effect in the **Object Name** field.

3. In the **Object Type** field, specify the type of object to which it will be applied.

4. Select **Create New**, click on **OK**, and the Wave Editor is displayed.

5. Click on **Record** when you are ready to record your sound. Click on **Stop** when you are done. Click on **Play** to hear what you have recorded.

N O T E

You must have a microphone and sound-capturing sound board to use this effect.

Adding Cues to an Animation

Cues control the playback of your animation. A cue controls the conditions that must be met before a specific action takes place. To add a cue:

1. Select the Cue tool from the toolbox. The Cue Information dialog box is displayed.

2. Enter a name, frame information, and condition for the cue.

3. Click on **OK**.

Summary

In this chapter you learned the elements of the CorelMOVE screen. You also learned how to create and use libraries; how to create, place, and animate objects; and how to play an animation.

Chapter 15

CorelVentura

CorelVentura is a powerful desktop publishing application that produces an incredible variety of documents. CorelVentura is fully compatible with previous Ventura Publisher (the former name of the program) files and is fully integrated with the rest of the CorelDRAW modules.

CorelVentura, formerly known as Ventura Publisher, was recently purchased by Corel Corp. and has been rewritten to conform to Windows and CorelDRAW standards. The new interface includes features such as roll-up menus and tabbed dialog boxes, as well as conformity to Windows text-editing standards. Other improvements include irregular text wrap around, rotation of text and objects on 0.1° increments, a faster built-in copy editor, access to all CorelDRAW shapes, and advanced color and prepress features. Due to considerations of space, this chapter covers only some of the basic operations of CorelVentura:

- ❖ Ventura basics
- ❖ File management
- ❖ Working with text
- ❖ Working with graphics

Ventura Basics

Start CorelVentura as you would any other CorelDRAW application: Double-click on its icon in the Corel 5 group. You'll see the starting screen shown in Figure 15.1.

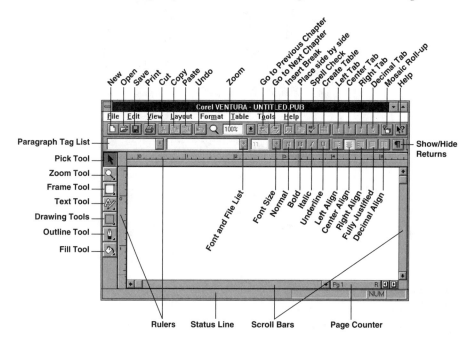

FIGURE 15.1 The CorelVentura screen.

❖   The **ribbon bar**, which is similar to the other ribbon bars in the CorelDRAW modules, lets you access the most frequently used Ventura features with the click of a button.

   – The **toolbox** contains the following tools:

   – The **Pick** tool to select and manipulate frames.

   – The **Zoom** tool to change the view of your document.

   – The **Frame** tool to add text or graphic frames.

   – The **Text** tool to add and edit text.

   – The **Paragraph** tool to format paragraphs of text.

- The **Drawing** tool to draw shapes.
- The **Outline** tool to create outlines for objects.
- The **Fill** tool to create fills for objects.

  As with other CorelDRAW modules, you may select a docked or floating toolbox from the View menu.
- The **rulers** are helpful for positioning objects on your pages. You may toggle the Ruler feature on and off through the View menu.
- The **scroll bars** work as in any other Windows applications: Click on the arrows to scroll incrementally or use the elevator buttons to move in larger increments.
- The **base page frame** is the underlying frame that usually holds the main text of the document.
- The **column guides** are nonprinting dashed lines that show you the edges of text columns.
- The **page counter** displays the current page number and whether the current page is a left page or a right page. To the right of the page information are scroll bars to move through the pages in the current chapter.
- The **status line** provides information about the currently selected object (as with CorelDRAW). It also provides information about the ribbon button or tool over which your mouse is currently positioned.

File Management

CorelVentura documents are controlled by a chapter file, which contains information on how the various elements of a document are combined. The chapter file keeps track of the graphics files, text files, and style sheets that combine to create a Ventura document. You may combine several chapter files into a publication file.

Creating a New Document

Select **New** from the File menu to create a new document. The New Publication dialog box, shown in Figure 15.2, is displayed.

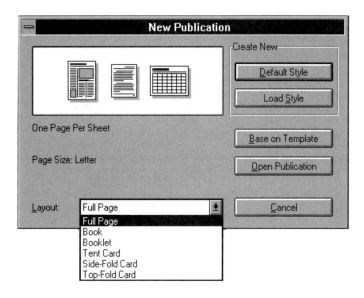

FIGURE 15.2 The New Publication dialog box

From the Layout pop-up menu, select the type of page layout you want:

❖ **Full Page**

❖ **Book**

❖ **Booklet**

❖ **Tent Card**

❖ **Side-Fold Card**

❖ **Top-Fold Card**

The preview box shows a representation of the layout you have selected. Click on **Default Style** to create the new document.

To create a document from a template, click on **Base on Template**. Then select a template file before you click on **Default Style**.

Opening an Existing Document

To open an existing document, select **Open** from the File menu. Then select the document from the standard Windows open dialog box and click on **OK**.

Getting Around in a Document

To get from one page to another in a CorelVentura document, use the scroll arrows on the page counter.

To go to a specific page, select **Go To** from the View menu, and you'll see the dialog box shown in Figure 15.3. Enter the page number in the **Page** field and click on the Go to Page button, or use the arrows at the top of the dialog box.

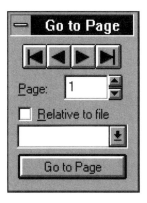

FIGURE 15.3 *The Go to Page dialog box*

Saving a Document

Use the **Save** command under the File menu to open the Save Publication As dialog box, which is shown in Figure 15.4. Enter the name of your file, select a directory location, and then click on **OK** to save the file.

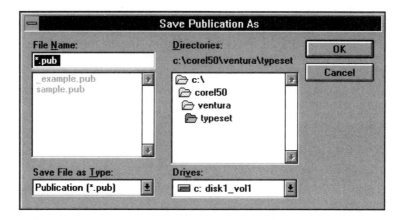

FIGURE 15.4 The Save Publication As dialog box

To save a document using a new name, select **Save As** from the File menu, enter a new name and location in the Save Publication As dialog box, and click on **OK**.

Viewing a Document

CorelVentura has three ways to display a document. They are all available from the View menu.

❖ **Page Layout** view is the default display mode, showing you how your document will look when you print it.

❖ **Draft** view looks similar to Page Layout view, except it "grays out" graphics so that your pages display faster.

❖ **Copy Editor** view displays your text in a single font so that you can edit your text quickly and your screen does not have to redraw graphics or multiple fonts. The panel on the left in the Copy Editor displays the names of the style tags for each paragraph.

When in Page Layout view or Draft view, you can use the Zoom tool to display the pages at different sizes. Click on the Zoom tool icon on the toolbar to display the Zoom tool pop-up menu shown in Figure 15.5.

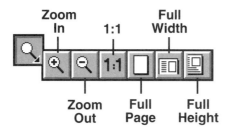

FIGURE 15.5 *The Zoom tool pop-up menu*

Printing a Document

To print a document, select **Print** from the File menu. You'll see the dialog box shown in Figure 15.6. Select whether you want to print the entire publication, the current chapter, the current page, or a range of pages, as well as the number of copies to print. You can also select your printer and print resolution from this dialog box. To access additional options, click on the Options button (for additional printing options) or the Setup button (for the standard Windows Print Setup dialog box)and make your selections. When you have selected all your printing options, click on **OK**.

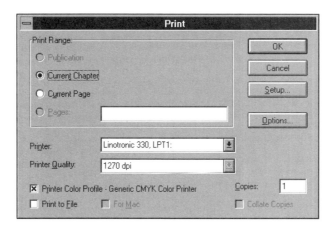

FIGURE 15.6 *The Print dialog box*

Frames

Text and graphics must be placed in containers, or *frames*, in CorelVentura. Each document has at least one frame: the base page frame, which is usually used for the main text of the document. Frames also hold graphics, captions, footnotes, headers, and footers.

WARNING

Each frame can hold one file. If you select a frame that already holds a file (text or graphic), choose another file for the frame. The new file will replace the first one.

There are five types of frames you can use.

❖ **Base page frames** are the underlying frames that usually hold the main text. Text placed in base page frames automatically flows from one page to the next. You can change the specifications of the base page frame by selecting **Chapter Settings** from the Layout menu.

❖ **Free frames**, unlike base page frames, are created with the Frame tool and can be moved (using the Pick tool) anywhere on the page. They can also be anchored in text so that they flow with selected text. Free frames are good for holding imported graphics, holding call outs, creating white space on a page, and laying out text for newsletters and magazines. To create a Free frame, select the Frame tool and then click and drag where you want the frame to go.

❖ **Caption frames** are created by CorelVentura when you add a caption to a free frame. The caption is linked to the free frame and moves with it.

❖ **Header and Footer** frames are produced by CorelVentura when you create headers or footers for a document. These frames automatically adjust according to the size of the text.

❖ **Footnote** frames are created by CorelVentura to hold footnote text.

Use your Pick tool to move and resize frames (other than base page frames). To change the specifications of a frame, select the frame you want to edit; then select **Frame** from the Format menu. Make your selections in the Frame Settings dialog box and click on **OK**.

Object Linking and Embedding

When you import a file, the link is static. This means that if the imported file needs to be updated. You must leave CorelVentura, open the file's source application, make your changes, export the file to a format compatible with Ventura, and then repeat the original import function. With OLE, however, you can actively edit the imported file while still in CorelVentura. OLE is a feature of Microsoft Windows that allows files to be dynamically linked.

To insert an object using OLE:

1. Select the frame you want to hold the object; then choose **Insert Object** from the Edit menu. You'll see the Insert Object dialog box shown in Figure 15.7.

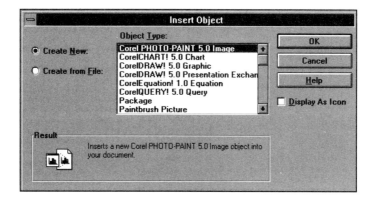

FIGURE 15.7 The Insert Object dialog box

2. To create a source document, choose **Create New** and select the source application used to create the object you wish to insert. That application will launch, and you can create the file to be inserted in your document.

You may also insert an existing file. Choose **Create from File**, select the source application, and choose the existing file to insert into your document.

N O T E

3. Click on **OK** to open the source application.

4. When the source application is initiated, create a new file or select an existing one to embed in CorelDRAW.

5. To later edit your embedded file, select the object in your CorelDRAW file and then choose the name of the file after you select **Object** on the Edit menu.

Text

You may add text directly into CorelVentura or import text from other word processing programs. Once you have your text in your CorelVentura document, you have some powerful editing features available to you, including a spelling checker and a thesaurus, as well as many formatting options.

You can enter and edit text in any view mode, however, the Copy Editor mode is definitely the most efficient choice. Unless you have a specific reason for editing text in Page Layout or Draft modes, you should use the Copy Editor mode, which is shown in Figure 15.8.

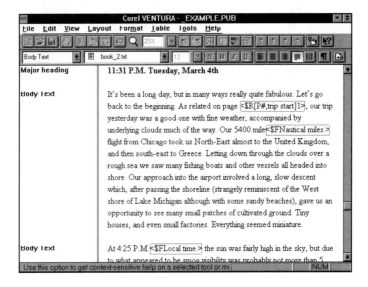

FIGURE 15.8 The Copy Editor viewing mode

Entering Text

To enter text directly into CorelVentura, select the Text tool, click in a frame, select **Copy Editor** from the View menu (unless you have a good reason not to), and begin typing. The Copy Editor works just like a basic word processing program, and you have access to the ribbon bar for formatting.

Text from Other Sources

To import text from most popular word processing programs, place your text cursor in the frame where you want to place your text. You may be in any view mode to do this, but if you are going to be formatting or editing this text, your best choice is Copy Editor view.

All paragraph formatting information (tab settings, indents, margins, etc.) is lost when you import text files, although specific character attributes (size, font, style, etc.) are kept.

N O T E

Select **Load Text** from the File menu, and you will see the dialog box. Select the word processing file you want to import. If you want to place the imported text at a particular location in existing text, place your cursor there and select **Insert at Cursor**. Click on **OK**.

Text Utilities

CorelVentura provides you with three very useful utilities: Spell Check, Thesaurus, and TypeAssist, all available at the top of the Tools menu.

❖ **Spell Check** checks the spelling in an entire document, or portions thereof, depending on the options you select in the Spell Check dialog box.

❖ **Thesaurus** finds synonyms for selected words. To look up a synonym, select the word you want to look up and then choose **Thesaurus** from the Tools menu. Follow the instructions in the dialog box to look up and replace words.

❖ **TypeAssist** automatically corrects typing errors such as capitalization, quotation marks, and spelling errors. From the TypeAssist dialog box, select the items you want to correct, along with the appropriate options, and then click on **OK**.

Formatting Text

You can format text in any of the three view modes, but, again, your best choice is probably the Copy Editor mode.

You have three main ways to format text:

❖ **Character formatting**. Select the text you want to format; then choose your formatting options from the ribbon bar. You may also choose the **Selected Text** option from the Format menu to display the Text Attributes dialog box, but the ribbon bar is much more expedient.

❖ **Style tags**. Using style tags is a quick and easy way to format large documents, or documents that use many different styles for different paragraphs. Style tags apply to selected paragraphs a tag that indicates the formatting for that paragraph (this feature is sometimes known as a style sheet in other popular software).

Select **Tags Roll-Up** from the Tools menu to display the current style tag list. Click anywhere in the paragraph you want to apply a tag to and then select the tag from the roll-up menu.

❖ To add or edit the existing tag list, select **Manage Tag List** from the Format menu.

– To add a tag, click on **Add Tag** and name your new style tag.

– To edit an existing or added tag, select the tag you want to edit, click on **Edit Tags** and then select the text and paragraph attributes you want. Click on **OK** when you are through.

– To delete a tag, select the tag name and click on **Delete Tag**.

Click on **Close** when you are through.

❖ **Local formatting**. This is a combination between style tags and character formatting. Local formatting is applied to style-tagged text when you want to make one-of-a-kind changes that don't require the creation of a new tag. Select the tagged text you want to format; then follow the instructions for character formatting.

Adding Headers and Footers

To add headers and footers, select **Chapter Settings** from the Layout menu. In the Chapter Settings dialog box, select the Header/Footer tab, shown in Figure 15.9.

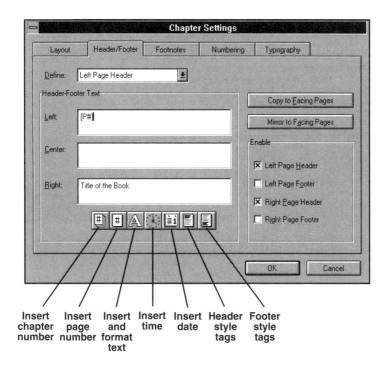

FIGURE 15.9 The Header/Footer tab in the Chapter Settings dialog box

From the **Define** list, select whether you are creating a header or footer for the left or right page. Add the text in the **Left**, **Center**, or **Right** text field, depending on where in the header or footer you want your text displayed. Use the buttons at the bottom of the dialog box to add chapter numbers, page numbers, date, time, and formatting to your header or footer text. Click on **OK** when you are done.

Graphics

You can place graphics created in any of the CorelDRAW modules, as well as clip art, photos, and art from most other graphics packages to liven up your CorelVentura documents. You can also create simple graphic elements (lines, ellipses, and squares) using CorelVentura's drawing tools.

The Drawing Tools

All CorelVentura's drawing tools are available from the Drawing Tool pop-up menu on the toolbar, shown in Figure 15.10.

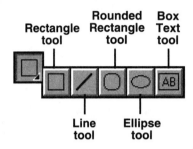

FIGURE 15.10 *Ventura's drawing tools*

Use the Pick tool to select the frame your shape will be attached to. Click on the tool you want to draw with and then click and drag your cursor. When you get the desired shape, release your mouse. Use the Pick tool to edit your shapes, if needed.

The Box Text tool creates a box into which you can type text. The box can then be moved and manipulated. The text in a box text object is formatted using the default BOXTEXT style tag. To change the formatting of the text, follow the steps to edit that tag.

Importing Graphics

To import graphics into CorelVentura, select a frame in which to place the graphic; then choose **Load Graphic** from the File menu. If you do not select a frame in which to place your graphic, CorelVentura automatically creates a frame the size of the graphic you are importing.

From the Load Graphic dialog box shown in Figure 15.11, select the file you want to import and then click on **OK**.

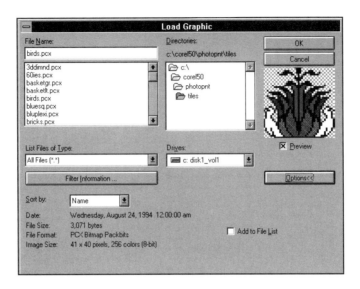

FIGURE 15.11 The Load Graphic dialog box with Preview enabled

You may also import graphics from the Mosaic Roll-Up, found under the File menu. See Chapter 9 for instruction on how to use Mosaic.

To manipulate the attributes of a graphic, such as its size, select the graphic and then select **Graphic** from the Format menu. The Frame Settings dialog box is displayed with the Graphic tab selected. Enter your specifications in the dialog box; then click on **OK**.

Running Text Around a Graphic

To run text around a graphic, select the frame with the Pick tool; then select **Frame** from the Format menu. Under the General tab, select **Flow Text Around Frame**.

Adding Captions

To add a caption to your graphic, select the frame with the Pick tool and then select **Frame** from the Format menu. Under the General tab, select the placement of the caption (above, below, left, or right) from the Caption pop-up menu. Click on the Text tool icon (the A) to add text and apply character attributes. The **Reference** option automatically inserts and numbers figures and tables.

Appendix A: Keyboard Shortcuts

Commands

CorelDRAW Commands	Global Windows Commands
Undo	Alt-Backspace
To Pick State	Ctrl-Spacebar
To Front	Shift-PgUp
To Back	Shift-PgDn
Forward One	Ctrl-PgUp
Back One	Ctrl-PgDn
Redo	Alt-Enter
Paste	Shift-Insert
Cut	Shift-Delete
Copy	Ctrl-Insert

CorelDRAW!

File Menu

Menu Option	Keyboard Shortcut
New	Ctrl-N
Open	Ctrl-O
Save	Ctrl-S
Mosaic Roll-Up	Alt-F1
Print	Ctrl-P
Exit	Alt-F4

Edit menu

Menu Option	Keyboard Shortcut
Undo	Ctrl-Z
Redo	Alt-Enter
Repeat	Ctrl-R
Cut	Ctrl-X
Copy	Ctrl-C
Paste	Ctrl-V
Delete	Del
Duplicate	Ctrl-D

Layout Menu

Menu Option	Keyboard Shortcut
Layers Roll-Up	Ctrl-F3
Styles Roll-Up	Ctrl-F5
Snap To Grid	Ctrl-Y

Effects menu

Menu Option	Keyboard Shortcut
Rotate & Skew	Alt-F5
Stretch & Mirror	Alt-F9
Envelope Roll-Up	Ctrl-F7
Blend Roll-Up	Ctrl-B
Extrude Roll-Up	Ctrl-E
Contour Roll-Up	Ctrl-F9
Powerline Roll-Up	Ctrl-F8
Lens Roll-Up	Alt-F3

Text menu

Menu Option	Keyboard Shortcut
Text Roll-Up	Ctrl-F2
Character	Ctrl-T
Fit Text To Path	Ctrl-F
Align To Baseline	Alt-F10
Edit Text	Ctrl-Shift-T

Arrange Menu

Menu Option	Keyboard Shortcut
Move	Alt-F7
Align	Ctrl-A
Group	Ctrl-G
Ungroup	Ctrl-U
Combine	Ctrl-L
Break Apart	Ctrl-K
Convert To Curves	Ctrl-Q
To Front	Shift-PgUp
To Back	Shift-PgDn
Forward One	Ctrl-PgUp
Back One	Ctrl-PgDn

View Menu

Menu Option	Keyboard Shortcut
Wireframe	Shift F9
Refresh Window	Ctrl-W
Full-Screen Preview	F9

Special Menu

Menu Option	Keyboard Shortcut
Preferences	Ctrl-J
Symbols Roll-Up	Ctrl-F11
Presets Roll-Up	Alt-F5

Help Menu

Menu Option	Keyboard Shortcut
Contents	F1
Screen/Menu Help	Shift-F1
Search For Help On	Ctrl-F1

CorelCHART!

Chart Mode

Menu Option	Keyboard Shortcut
Bold	Ctrl-B
Italic	Ctrl-I
Underline	Ctrl-U

File Menu

Menu Option	Keyboard Shortcut
New	Ctrl-N
Open	Ctrl-O

Save	Ctrl-S
Print	Ctrl-P
Preferences	Ctrl-J
Exit	Alt-F4

Edit Menu

Menu Option	Keyboard Shortcut
Undo	Ctrl-Z
Cut	Ctrl-X
Copy	Ctrl-C
Paste	Ctrl-V
Delete	Del
Duplicate	Ctrl-D

Arrange Menu

Menu Option	Keyboard Shortcut
To Front	Shift-PgUp
To Back	Shift-PgDn
Forward One	PgUp
Back One	PgDn
Align	Ctrl-A

Window Menu

Menu Option	Keyboard Shortcut
Cascade	Shift-F5
Tile Vertically	Shift-F4

Help Menu

Menu Option	Keyboard Shortcut
Contents	F1
Screen/Menu Help	Shift-F1
Search For Help On	Ctrl-F1

File Menu

Menu Option	Keyboard Shortcut
New	Ctrl-N
Open	Ctrl-O
Save	Ctrl-S
Print Preview	F9
Print	Crtl-P
Exit	Alt-F4

Edit Menu

Menu Option	Keyboard Shortcut
Undo	Ctrl-Z
Cut	Ctrl-X
Copy	Ctrl-C
Paste	Ctrl-V

Format Menu

Menu Option	Keyboard Shortcut
Numeric	Ctrl-0 (zero)
Font	Ctrl-F

Alignment   Ctrl-A

Get Page Break   Ctrl-Q

Data Menu

Menu Option	Keyboard Shortcut
Find Next	F3
Find Prev	Shift-F3
Enter Formula	F12

Options Menu

Menu Option	Keyboard Shortcut
Display Grid	Ctrl-G
Auto Recalc	Shift-F7
Recalc Now	F7

Window Menu

Menu Option	Keyboard Shortcut
Cascade	Shift-F5
Tile Vertically	Shift-F4

Help Menu

Menu Option	Keyboard Shortcut
Contents	F1
Screen/Menu Help	Shift-F1
Search For Help On	Ctrl-F1

CorelMOSAIC!

File Menu

Menu Option	Keyboard Shortcut
New Collection	Ctrl-N
Open Collection	Ctrl-O
Preferences	Ctrl-J
Exit	Alt-F4

Window Menu

Menu Option	Keyboard Shortcut
Cascade	Shift-F5
Tile Vertically	Shift-F4

Help Menu

Menu Option	Keyboard Shortcut
Contents	F1
Screen/Menu Help	Shift-F1
Search For Help On	Ctrl-F1

CorelMOVE!

File Menu

Menu Option	Keyboard Shortcut
New	Ctrl-N
Open	Ctrl-O

Save	Ctrl-S
Mosaic Roll-Up	Alt-F1
Exit	Alt-F4

Edit Menu

Menu Option	Keyboard Shortcut
Cut	Ctrl-X
Copy	Ctrl-C
Delete	Del
Duplicate	Ctrl-D
Animation Info	Ctrl-A

View Menu

Menu Option	Keyboard Shortcut
First Frame	Shift-F5
Last Frame	Shift-F6
Next Frame	Shift-F8
Previous Frame	Shift-F7
Play	F9
Stop	Esc

Arrange Menu

Menu Option	Keyboard Shortcut
To Front	Shift-PgUp
To Back	Shift-PgDn
Forward One	Ctrl-PgUp
Back One	Ctrl-PgDn

View Menu

Menu Option	Keyboard Shortcut
Play	F9
Stop	Esc

Help Menu

Menu Option	Keyboard Shortcut
Contents	F1
Screen/Menu Help	Shift-F1
Search For Help On	Ctrl-F1

CorelPHOTO-PAINT!

File Menu

Menu Option	Keyboard Shortcut
New	Ctrl-N
Open	Ctrl-O
Save	Ctrl-S
Print	Ctrl-P
Exit	Alt-F4

Edit Menu

Menu Option	Keyboard Shortcut
Undo	Ctrl-Z
Cut	Ctrl-X

Copy	Ctrl-C
Paste	Ctrl-V

View Menu

Menu Option	Keyboard Shortcut
100% (No Zoom)	Ctrl-1
Canvas Roll-Up	F3
Color Roll-Up	F2
Fill Roll-Up	F6
Tool Settings Roll-Up	F8
Full Screen Preview	F9

Special Menu

Menu Option	Keyboard Shortcut
Preferences	Ctrl-J

Window Menu

Menu Option	Keyboard Shortcut
Cascade	Shift-F5
Tile Vertically	Shift-F4
Refresh	Ctrl-W
Duplicate	Ctrl-D

Help Menu

Menu Option	Keyboard Shortcut
Contents	F1
Search for Help on	Ctrl-F1

CorelSHOW!

File Menu

Menu Option	Keyboard Shortcut
New	Ctrl-N
Open	Ctrl-O
Save	Ctrl-S
Mosaic Roll-Up	Alt-F1
Print	Ctrl-P
Run Screen Show	Ctrl-F5
Preferences	Ctrl-J
Exit	Alt-F4

Edit Menu

Menu Option	Keyboard Shortcut
Cut	Ctrl-X
Copy	Ctrl-C
Paste	Ctrl-V
Delete	Del

Insert Menu

Menu Option	Keyboard Shortcut
Slide	Ctrl-G
Object	Ctrl-D
Animation	Ctrl-A
Sound	Ctrl-Y

Arrange Menu

Menu Option	Keyboard Shortcut
To Front	Shift-PgUp
To Back	Shift-PgDn
Forward One	Ctrl-PgUp
Back One	Ctrl-PgDn
To Fit Object To Slide	F4

Window Menu

Menu Option	Keyboard Shortcut
Cascade	Shift-F5
Refresh Window	Ctrl-W
Tile Vertically	Shift-F4

Help Menu

Menu Option	Keyboard Shortcut
Contents	F1
Screen/Menu Help	Shift-F1
Search For Help On	Ctrl-F1

CorelTRACE!

File Menu

Menu Option	Keyboard Shortcut
Open	Ctrl-O
Save Trace	Ctrl-S
Exit	Alt-F4

Edit Menu

Menu Option	Keyboard Shortcut
Undo	Ctrl-Z
Cut	Ctrl-X
Copy	Ctrl-C
Paste	Ctrl-V
Delete	Del

View Menu

Menu Option	Keyboard Shortcut
Refresh Window	Ctrl-W

Help menu

Menu Option	Keyboard Shortcut
Contents	F1
Screen/Menu Help	Shift-F1
Search For Help On...	Ctrl-F1

Index

333